Problem-Based Case Learning: Making Learning Real with Educators, Businesses, and Students in Partnership

by
Jim Johnson, Ed.D.
Ruth Loring, Ph.D.

Contributing Authors:

John Bransford, Ph.D.
Nancy Vye, Ph.D.
Dale Rogers, M. Ed.
Ted Kraus, M. Ed.

Phyllis Gobbell, Editor

Problem-Based Case Learning:
Making Learning Real
with Educators, Businesses,
and Students in Partnership

Cover by: Dale Rogers & Kristy Johnson
Page Composition & Typography by: Kristy Johnson

ISBN: 1466304863
ISBN-13: 978-1466304864

Website
www.makinglearningreal.org
Email: staff@makinglearningreal.org

Dedicated to:

Ruth Loring

ABOUT THE AUTHORS

Jim Johnson

Jim Johnson has been the Principle Investigator for Innovations in Teaching and Learning for Advanced Technology Education. Prior to this project, he was the Principle Investigator for The Case Files and a member of the advisory board for the Center for Information Technology Education (CITE), a Regional NSF Center. In 2009, he retired as Dean of Technology at Nashville State Community College (NSCC) where he directed these projects as well as led all two-year AAS and AS technology programs. Prior to joining the staff at NSCC, Jim had varied career spanning both education and business. He taught physics and led a two-year AAS program in Laser Technology before joining the Project Management staff at Control Laser Corp, an industrial laser manufacturer. He established and for 12 years, operated Photon Dynamics Inc., a laser consulting and laser safety organization. He joined the staff of CORD in Waco, Texas as a Senior Project Manager in charge of all post-secondary projects. During this time he completed a Doctor of Education Degree at Baylor University. His varied career in business and education has had a major influence on the design and outcome of the projects he has directed.

Jim now lives, in partial retirement, in Nashville where he and his wife Judy enjoy time with grandchildren. He is an active member of Gideon's International and enjoys traveling and fishing whenever possible.

Ruth Loring

With nearly forty years as an educator, Ruth Loring has extensive and in-depth experience that includes teaching, supervising, consulting, writing, and translating the principles of "how people learn" into practice. She earned a Ph.D. and M.ED. in Reading at the University of North Texas and a B.A. from Baylor University. She has conducted research of the impact of school-to-career programs and developed approaches to integrating curriculum that connects school to the workplace and community through experiential, problem-based learning. Dr. Loring has a long history of collaboration with other educators in the movement to teach skillful thinking throughout the curriculum. An enthusiastic proponent of problem-based case learning (PBCL), she served as Professional Development specialist at Nashville State Community College to design and implement professional development activities for faculty involved in The Case Files, CITE, and the IT Academy projects. As Senior Project leader, she led implementation of the NSF-funded project, Innovation in Teaching and Learning for Technological Education (ITLTE).

It has been her great passion to share her knowledge and experience with problem-based learning in a document such as this.

CONTENTS

ACKNOWLEDGMENTS

by Jim Johnson
Nashville State Community College

When I joined the staff at Nashville State Community College (NSCC), Sydney Rogers, Vice President of Outreach Services, met me at the door. I had talked with her during my employment interview and realized that she had submitted two proposals to the National Science Foundation (NSF) Advanced Technological Education (ATE) program. Within the first week of my tenure at NSCC, Sydney confirmed that NSF would be honoring us with both grants.

The new grants would continue with the work started during two previous grants. She also confirmed that I would be the Principal Investigator on one of the grants and a member of the Oversight Committee for the other. These two new grants would build upon the knowledge and successes gained in the first two grants by expanding, developing and documenting the effectiveness of the process defined as Problem-Based Case Learning (PBCL). As the new Dean of Technology, I saw educational challenges that I wanted to start to work on within the Business and Technology Division, and these grants provided that opportunity.

A concluding grant was provided by NSF in 2008, to use web-based video as a dissemination format. Thus, with the oversight of Dr. Gerhard Salinger at NSF and the technical guidance of Dr. John Bransford and his team of experts from the University of Washington (formerly associated with Vanderbilt University), NSCC has dedicated nearly fifteen years of project work funded by NSF to the implementation of PBCL in a growing number of technically orientated courses at community colleges across the nation.

For documentation purposes the sequence of the NSF grants is as follows:

- TEFATE (Tennessee Exemplary Faculty for Advanced Technological Education)
- SEATEC (Southeast Advanced Technological Education Consortium)
- The Case Files
- CITE (The Regional Center for Information Technology Education)Synergy Conferences 1, 2, and 3
- ITLTE (Innovations in Teaching and Learning for Technological Education)

PBCL, which will be explained in greater detail, begins with a business partner and the teacher working together to define a "problem" to be presented to the class. The problem needs to be a current, authentic situation that is meaningful to the business partner and to the students but not in the "critical path" of business operations. Not all business problems can be used for this type of instruction. Thus a close working relationship must exist between the teacher and the business partner for PBCL to be most effective.

To solve this type of problem situation, students must integrate their past knowledge and experiences, academic skills learned in previous classes, and technical skills. When students work in teams to integrate these three elements, they can obtain potential problem solutions for the business partner. No technical problem has only one solution and thus different groups of students may propose vastly different solutions to the same problem. When the students believe they have a meaningful solution to propose, the business partner is invited to listen to their proposed solutions and to help the teacher evaluate the solutions.

Frequently, teachers feel the obligation of "teaching" technical information before students experience it. However, it has been found that a teacher lecturing on an issue is often not the most effective teaching method. All students come to the class with preconceived ideas based on their past experiences. Allowing the students to use their past experiences to help solve a problem is an extremely effective learning method. More details regarding the learning processes associated with PBCL are included in the following chapters.

Making learning real and relevant for the student is the ultimate purpose of the grant provided by NSF. Hundreds of faculty members from STEM disciplines in colleges across the nation have learned the PBCL process during the course of these projects. As a result, well over 1000 students have experienced PBCL in their classrooms. Feedback data from teachers, students and employers have expressed the benefits of the PBCL process.

Some of the comments from students and teachers are related to the fact that students can use their past experiences to help solve current problems and that teamwork which is vital to all businesses today is experienced on a first hand basis by students using the PBCL process. Employers have commented that students who have experienced the PBCL process reach productivity levels at their new job much faster than other students and that they have an enhanced ability to solve problems and to be productive in multidisciplinary teams.

In addition to Sydney Rogers, Dr. John Bransford, and Dr. Gerhard Salinger, there are large numbers of teachers, students and administrators responsible for the success and dissemination of PBCL. Far too many educators have contributed to this work to be individually mentioned. Dr. George Van Allen, President, and Dr. Ellen Weed, Vice President for Academic Affairs, at Nashville State Community College have given their complete support and assistance with each of the grants described above. Without their encouragement little could have been accomplished.

David McNeel was another key member of the project staff. As the Director of CITE Regional Center, he helped spread the PBCL concept around the state and to several Tennessee high schools. In addition, he spent countless hours structuring the three Synergy Conferences held in Nashville in 2004, Boston in 2006, and in Phoenix in 2008, which exposed hundreds of teachers to the PBCL process.

Many faculty members at NSCC have worked on the development and implementation of PBCL. Innocent Usoh, Jim Graf, Ed Mummert, Beverly Bradley, Michelle Lenox, Judy Kane, Bill Finney, Jack Wallace, Bill Kitchen, Susan Jones, Dale Rogers, and Ted Kraus are teachers at NSCC who have developed and pilot tested many of the PBCL learning modules. These individuals all worked extra time to learn the PBCL process and revise their classes to implement the new process. Since The Case Files project, one individual stands out as the champion of the cause, in this case developing and implementing the PBCL process.

That individual for the last series of projects is Dr. Ruth Loring. In 2001, when I learned that I was selected as the project director, my thoughts immediately went to Dr. Loring, with whom I had worked several years before. She came to Nashville at my request and became acquainted with the PBCL process and the individuals working on the grants. She was so intrigued by the concept that she soon left her consulting work and joined the project staff on a full time basis. She concentrated her efforts on professional development for teachers and on the PBCL substance incorporated in the project web site: www.makinglearningreal.org

Partners on the final Innovations in Teaching and Learning for Technological Education dissemination grant include WGBH, the Educational Broadcasting organization in Boston. Administrators, planners, and technical staff from WGBH worked tirelessly using their wealth of experience to develop the project web site. This site provides teachers with an overview of PBCL that will allow them to begin using the process in their classes.

An entire staff at WGBH participated in the project, which was led by Amy Tonkonogy and Arthur Smith. Another partner during dissemination of PBCL has been the Midwest Center for Information Technology (MCIT) a coalition of ten institutions in Nebraska, Iowa, North Dakota, and South Dakota. Colleges in many states have implemented PBCL in several classes, states including Texas, Virginia, California, Massachusetts, Nevada, Alabama, Arkansas, California, Colorado, Connecticut, Florida, Illinois, Kentucky, Louisiana, Maryland, Mississippi, Minnesota, Missouri, North Carolina, New Hampshire, Nevada, New York, Ohio, Pennsylvania, South Carolina, Washington, West Virginia, and Wyoming.

In several cases the PBCL concept has been modified and adapted for local variations. As a network of colleges, teachers and learners develop, it is very difficult to record all the states, teachers and students that have become part of the process.

As the Principal Investigator for this series of projects, I sincerely hope that you will investigate the PBCL process in depth and that you will be encouraged to identify a business partner to help you structure a PBCL activity for your class. Project staff remains available for training activities at your college or for mentoring assistance as you integrate PBCL in your course content and learning processes.

FOREWORD

by John Bransford and Nancy Vye
College of Education-University of Washington

Contributing Author, Dr. John D. Bransford joined the College of Education-University of Washington in Seattle in 2003 where he holds the Shauna C. Larson Endowed Chair in Learning Sciences. He previously served as Centennial Professor of Psychology and Education and Co-director of the Learning Technology Center at Vanderbilt University. Author of seven books and hundreds of articles and presentations, Bransford is an internationally renowned scholar in cognition and technology. His research in the 1970s in the areas of human learning, memory, and problem solving helped to shape the "cognitive revolution." He served as Co-Chair of the National Academy of Science committee that wrote "How People Learn: Brain Mind, Experience and School" and "How People Learn, Bridging Research and Practice".

Contributing Author, Nancy Vye, Ph.D, is a Principal Research Scientist in the College of Education at the University of Washington. She received her doctorate in cognitive psychology from Vanderbilt University and was Co-Director of the Learning Technology Center at Vanderbilt. Her research has focused on challenge-based learning and formative assessment in classroom settings. Vye's research and development work includes The Arts for Learning Lessons Project, an arts-integrated literacy curriculum for elementary students; The Adventures of Jasper Woodbury, a mathematics problem solving series; Schools for Thought, a technology-based, educational reform initiative; Betty's Brain, a pedagogical computer agent that teaches cause-effect reasoning; and STARLegacy software that supports problem-based learning.

The contributors to this volume, the majority of whom are leaders in community colleges across the nation, discuss examples of an innovative community-centered approach to teaching and learning that represents a win/win/win opportunity for students, instructors, and local businesses to learn by working together and making a difference in the world.

The work discussed in this book has been evolving for some time. One of the salient beginning points for this evolutionary path involved production of The Case Files. (See www.thecasefiles.org.) A National Science Foundation/ Advanced Technological Education project, The Case Files is a set of multimedia course materials that were implemented in a number of community college classrooms and are still used by many people. We, along with several other colleagues from the learning sciences, had the pleasure of working with (and learning from) members of The Case Files group during the early phases of their work. We remember vividly some of the cases developed. The work of The Case Files group built on earlier efforts by the South East Advanced Technological Education Consortium (SEATEC). One of the examples developed under SEATEC and brought under The Case Files umbrella was a real case of a bridge that collapsed while it was under construction. One worker was killed and many others were traumatized as they were hurled into the river below.

Understanding what went wrong in the case of the bridge collapse - it was caused by a lack of coordinated communication among the different groups of people doing the construction - provided important information that we as learning scientists (and novices with respect to bridge construction) have never forgotten. For example, we learned that major engineering activities like bridge design require a design for a stable final structure, but also a design for how to work with collaborative teams to erect a stable structure in the first place. A number of factors must be considered when creating both of these designs, including the geological history of the area (e.g., are there floods, earthquakes?), the materials used to build the bridge, the design of communication networks for the different teams working simultaneously on parts of the construction and needing to coordinate with one another, and so forth. It was during the erection of the structure that coordinated communication failed, ultimately leading to the collapse of the bridge. Information about other intriguing problems from The Case Files (e.g., how to design simple containers to keep pizzas hot) can be found at:

www.thecasefiles.org

Over time, the developers of The Case Files observed that learning from "already solved" cases (in the bridge example, engineers had already determined reasons for the collapse) was helpful for motivation and memory (seeing the cases certainly worked that way for us). However, there was often a lack of motivation by students to engage in the kinds of active and collaborative problem solving that can prepare people with more advanced skills, knowledge and attitudes for lifelong learning (e.g., Bransford & Schwartz, 1999; Kay & Greenhill, 2011). Like most busy people, community college students appreciated the cases but many said, essentially, "Just tell us what happened and why." Especially for community college students, many of whom have family duties and other jobs or may be desperately seeking the skills that will help them qualify for a new one as soon as possible, this request makes a great deal of sense.

The Case Files represented a strong beginning for improving instruction and learning, but its developers – in listening to students, local businesses, fellow community college instructors and other educators – realized that there were ways to make instruction even more effective. Chapter 2 explores in more detail the developmental history that led to the new learning environments design that is discussed in this volume. We discuss a part of that history in this Foreword because the information is important for setting the stage for the rest of this volume, and especially for explaining how this group's developmental process led to the name for the approach to teaching, learning and community building that represents the primary focus of this book.

Problem-Based Case Learning (PBCL)

The name of the instructional innovation discussed in this book is PBCL for "Problem-Based Case Learning." In our learning sciences literature, this name is unique. People have talked about problem-based learning, project-based learning, case-based learning, design-based learning, learning through goal-based scenarios, and other titles. Williams (1992) provides an excellent overview of how these approaches, while having some general similarities, also have distinct differences as well. Based on the literatures we knew, the idea of "Problem-Based Case Learning" was initially unfamiliar to us.

Thanks to the patience of our community college friends, it became clear to us how this name was very meaningful given the trajectories of its development. The original case files fit well with many examples of case-based learning (e.g. see Gragg, 1940; Williams, 1992), but recall that students were quite aware that the cases presented to them had already been solved (as noted earlier, for example, a major team had investigated the reasons for the bridge collapse). Students didn't want to reinvent the wheel by having to "guess" at the answers; they simply wanted to be told the answers.

The "problem-based" addition to the case file approach was designed, in part, to obviate requests from students to "just tell us the answer." Cases that were problem-based involved "unsolved problems" that did not have a worked out answer for a particular context of application. The only way to make progress was to work through the unsolved problems, and the latter were clearly authentic to the students and typically complex enough that they benefited from a collaborative approach by people with different kinds of experiences and expertise. Over time, the advantages of changing from "case-based learning" to (unsolved) Problem-Based Case Learning became meaningful to us and intriguingly generative.

Of course, a question that arises is: What does it mean to create cases that include "unsolved problems"? The major instructional mandate of the contributors to this book is to provide high quality technology education for their students. The cases they discuss in the context of PBCL involve work with actual clients: ideally, local businesses where particular community colleges reside. The unsolved problems could include requests from local business people such as "I need a better but less expensive way to advertise what is available in my little shop and to communicate with my customers." Or "Is there any way that I can use technology to take inventory so I don't have to shut down to do it?" Or "How can I effectively train new employees and keep everyone abreast of new policies?" Many businesses, especially small ones, cannot afford to hire consultants to help them learn to "work smarter." And for the students and instructors working to solve a problem, the need to adapt ideas to novel contexts provides rich and authentic opportunities for learning and innovation by all the partners (businesses, students, instructors) involved.

The Importance of America's Community Colleges

The fact that this book focuses on instructional innovations in community colleges is exciting and timely. In 2008, the College Board's Center for Innovative Thought published *"Winning the Skills Race and Strengthening America's Middle Class: An Action Agenda for Community Colleges"*. The report highlights the immensely important yet often overlooked role of community colleges in our nation's infrastructure of educational opportunities. The authors of the report state:

> American community colleges are the nation's most overlooked asset. As the United States confronts the challenges of globalization, two-year institutions are indispensable to the American future. . . . In the century since they were founded, community colleges have become the largest single sector of American higher education, with nearly 1,200 regionally accredited two-year colleges enrolling 6.5 million students annually for credit (nearly half of all American undergraduates) and another 5 million for noncredit courses. Students range in age from teenagers to octogenarians, annually taking courses in everything from English literature, biochemistry, and statistics to foreign languages, the arts, community development, emergency medical procedures, engine maintenance, and hazardous waste disposal. (p. 5)

As we will see in this volume, community colleges provide extremely important opportunities for technology training as well.

Community colleges have a long history of working with local businesses and other partners, but often the partners are used primarily to give guest lectures or as board members who advise faculty on programmatic concerns: for example, new skills that students will need when they "graduate" to the workforce. These are important and useful and still an important part of the work of the authors of this volume. But PBCL represents an additional way to work with partners that opens up a number of important opportunities, and presents some challenges as well.

Opportunities and Challenges for Teaching and Learning

Figure 1 contains a diagram of the PBCL process. The diagram is taken from the PBCL website (www.makinglearningreal.org), which leads people though the entire PBCL cycle. It is worthwhile to go through this cycle on the web; it provides detailed information about each step in the cycle and grounds the process in rich video-based descriptions and examples. The PBCL cycle begins with the "handshake" (between a business and community college instructors and students) that is shown at the bottom left of the diagram in Figure 1. The cycle is also discussed in Chapter 2 of this volume and in each of the case studies that are described later in this book.

Figure 1:
The PBCL Cycle

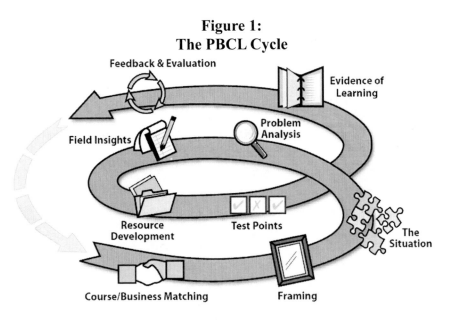

The fact that PBCL is based on real-world partnerships has a major impact on the kinds of teaching and learning processes that must take place to make it successful. First, PBCL is a general model that is designed to be adapted to particular settings; it is a framework for action, but not a closely scripted "one size fits all approach." This presents challenges for course instructors (e.g., How do I find a business partner?), but it also presents strong opportunities to change the nature of conversations about the role that community colleges play in our nation. PBCL helps community colleges become engines of innovation that are directly tied to benefits for the communities in which they do their work.

PBCL also changes what many call the "grammar of schooling," which often consists of lectures from experts, supervised labs (at least some of the time), and written tests (e.g., Parker, 2010). For PBCL to work, everyone needs to be a learner, not only students but also instructors and business partners. This can require significant shifts in the identities of the participants. For example, instructors need to become "adaptive experts" who know a lot but also are willing and adept at learning from others (including their students) and "on the fly." Hatano and colleagues' work on "adaptive expertise" is a very relevant concept for helping people rethink their identities and realize that PBCL requires new learning and innovation, not simply expert based telling (e.g., Hatano & Inagaki, 1986; Lin, Schwartz & Bransford, 2006; Bransford, 2007).

Other relevant readings include work by Miller (1978) on the behaviors of different kinds of information designers (e.g. artisans who typically keep applying a fixed set of templates to solve problems versus "virtuosos" who help clients reframe problems and invent ways to solve them on the fly). The books, *Corporate Creativity* (Robinson & Stern, 1998) and *The Mind at Work: Valuing the Intelligence of the American Worker* (Rose, 2004) are also very relevant because they help illuminate how an isolated "think-tank" approach to innovation can be far from optimal because it deprives groups of many insights that occur from workers who are close to the everyday work of a company or group (see Bransford et al., 2010). Work by Bereiter and Scardamalia (1993) also shows quite clearly the power of students - even K-12 students - to engage in the kinds of "knowledge building" that goes beyond the simple memorization of pre-digested content (although memorization can be important) when teachers provide opportunities for generating new knowledge and connections that are relevant to important problems that need to be solved (see Shutt, Phillips, Vye, Van Horne & Bransford, 2010).

PBCL also places a great deal of emphasis on assessment, especially formative assessment that provides ongoing feedback about the success of various activities. Bransford and Schwartz (2009) summarize many of the powerful findings in the expertise literature (e.g., Ericsson, 2009) by noting: "Practice makes permanent, not perfect." Only through well-orchestrated feedback mechanisms can we see how well we are doing and have chances to revise and improve. For PBCL, this includes monitoring student learning, instructor learning, and learning and satisfaction by the business partners. The assessments are not simply "tests" given for the purpose of assigning grades; they are sources of information for reflection and revision so that the quality of the PBCL experience is constantly improved.

As noted earlier, we have had the pleasure of working with and learning from many of the contributors to this volume for more than a decade. The progress they have made from the original (yet still valuable) work on The Case Files to the newer PBCL is exceptional and demonstrates their abilities to work as a large team. We have also had the pleasure of working with most of the authors of this volume as they have sought to tackle the challenges and opportunities of PBCL. They have had national meetings and frequent webinars, and we have had the opportunity to meet them and see firsthand how they work together.

Overall, PBCL is truly exciting and, because of the win/win/win nature of the concept and the motivation and innovative insights of the people involved in developing and working to bring it to scale, it seems clear that its influence will continue to grow.

This book provides an excellent opportunity to get a feel for PBCL by reading the fascinating range of case studies that are described.

This book is just the beginning, of course. Given our knowledge of the people involved, it seems clear that PBCL has an extremely bright future as a way to support socially-relevant learning and innovation in our country. This is especially true if one looks at the potential for introducing PBCL to other community colleges.

Figure 2 provides an illuminating view of the potential power of connecting the more than 1, 200 community colleges in our nation in ways that allow them to keep learning from one another. The exact number and location of community colleagues have probably changed some since this map was made available (American Association of Community Colleges, 2011).

However, even as an approximation, the map provides a stunning view of the ubiquity of community colleges in the United States.

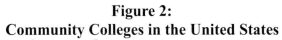

Figure 2:
Community Colleges in the United States

We are honored to have the opportunity to write this Foreword, and we thank all the authors for helping us think much more broadly about teaching, learning and connections to local communities. We look forward to further opportunities to learn by working with them.

(Preparation of this article was influenced by our colleagues in the LIFE Center and supported in part through a grant from the National Science Foundation (#0354453). However, the ideas expressed in this article are not necessarily those of the LIFE Center or the NSF.)

1

THE STORY BEHIND THE STORY

In the late 1990s, as instructors in technical education throughout the nation speculated on how to equip their students to enter the twenty-first century workforce, a group of teachers from Nashville State Technical Institute in Tennessee went out to visit local businesses and industries. Their objective was to determine what employers wanted, what knowledge and skills students needed in the "real world," and whether the college curriculum meshed with the workplace requirements.

One math instructor returned to the campus after a day at one company and said, "They don't use math."

But she went back and spent more time with the employer. After a few days, the instructor's perspective had changed. "They do use math," she said. "They just don't use it the way we teach it."

The push for improved technological education grew out of similar discoveries throughout the nation. Twenty-first century jobs require major changes in teaching strategies and subsequent redesign of course structures in engineering technology and information technology.

Business leaders are typically very interested in helping and advising for community college programs. The trick is to make certain there is effective communication with interested business partners. Most business leaders are willing to provide information about their business and to even give tours to the instructor so that the instructor will be better able to bring appropriate applications into student classes. Developing a close working relationship with an interested business partner or several partners from different businesses is one of the most important activities that teachers can engage in. The business connection allows teachers to bring the real world into the classroom and relate course activities to authentic business situations. From its starting point at Nashville State Technical Institute, now Nashville State Community College, **problem-based case learning (PBCL)** was at the heart of technical education reform. PBCL has since been implemented at colleges, universities, and high schools across the nation. (See Figure 2, Foreword).

PBCL is grounded in a variety of learner-centered approaches to teaching and learning: problem based learning, work based learning, project based learning, case based reasoning, experiential learning, scenario based and story centered curriculum, to name a few. In all these approaches, the learner constructs meaning through active engagement with concepts and skills set in context of use, while collaborating with others. Students must be actively engaged in their own learning process by remembering, creating, critiquing, and producing meaningful outcomes of what they know and are able to do – concepts discussed in greater detail by Art Costa, founder of The Institute for Habits of Mind. (See www.instituteforhabitsofmind.com.) The process both requires and develops complex communication and critical thinking skills as students learn to identify and solve uncharted problems.

From its origins more than a decade ago, PBCL has developed through several projects, each building on the other, modifying and refining the PBCL approach.

How the PBCL Process Developed

In 1998, the **Tennessee Exemplary Faculty for Advanced Technological Education (TEFATE)** project began with a goal to improve technological education through the development of a new Associate of Applied Science curriculum (A.A.S.) in communications technology. The development team explored ways in which faculty could learn to bring the workplace into the classroom.

The TEFATE project culminated in an unexpected additional outcome, the realization that case studies were being used in many educational programs for business, law, medicine, and education but in very few programs for technology. As a result, interdisciplinary project teams began to develop case studies for use in the communications technology curriculum. The work accomplished through the TEFATE project provided the necessary foundation for new models of development and use of case studies in technological education, becoming the precursor to PBCL.

In 1999, the **South East Advanced Technological Education Consortium (SEATEC)** project received funding to promote improvement in technological education through the design of case studies to be implemented in new curricula, instructional materials, and opportunities for faculty and teacher development. Critical goals of the project were to create a process that ensured students learn the necessary content, to incorporate ways to apply the content to real-world problems, and to encourage continuous learning as change occurs.

The SEATEC project team collaborated with business and industry partners to develop and field test a series of real-world model cases that reflected the needs of business as well as the needs of students. Four cases were produced by project partners at four different community colleges in Tennessee: The Case of the Gummies, I Want My Pizza Hot, TNSR69 Bridge Collapse, and A Netful of Work. (See References for more information.)

In addition, the SEATEC project team established a Learning Cycle as the structure for guiding students through working a case. This cycle, adapted by SEATEC for use in technological education, is based on a guided cyclical process developed and piloted at Vanderbilt University and the framework described in *How People Learn: Brain, Mind, Experience, and School*, published by the National Research Council. See References for more information.

The results of the SEATEC project demonstrated the benefits of the systematic approach to problem solving based on the Learning Cycle in collaboration with a business/industry partner.

Funded by NSF/ATE in 2002, The Case Files project leveraged the tools and processes developed during TEFATE and SEATEC. The Case Files project used the Learning Cycle as a design tool for faculty from across the nation to design, co-develop, and implement the innovative, student-centered teaching and learning process that came to be known as the Problem-Based Case Learning (PBCL) approach.

The **Case Files** project, led by Nashville State, with partners in Virginia, Arkansas, Ohio, Oklahoma, Nebraska, Iowa, and Massachusetts, developed case studies in engineering technology and information technology. Goals of the project were to generate an inventory of case studies as models for classroom use and to train faculty to develop their own cases. Supporting early predictions made by the evaluator of the TEFATE project, Roger Deveau, Professor, Department of Business Information Systems, University of Massachusetts at Dartmouth, The Case Files project has become "a catalyst for reforming the learning experience for students in engineering and information technology programs throughout the nation."

Also in 2002, **The Center for Information Technology Education (CITE)** was funded by NSF to focus on improving technological education through partnerships among secondary schools, community colleges, and business partners. These business/educator partnerships created the foundation for many of the early PBCL cases. CITE also sponsored or co-sponsored three national Synergy Conferences to help bring together all the various efforts to innovate in curriculum and instruction in community colleges.

The Corporate Scholars Solution (CSS) program, as part of CITE, was piloted in Spring 2003 and ran through Spring 2005. During this time 24 CSS projects were conducted, involving 19 employers and 333 students. Principal participants were faculty from two community colleges and two universities. The CSS program emphasized contextual learning.

Innovation in Teaching and Learning (ITL), a partnership of Nashville State Community College and WGBH Educational Foundation in Boston, began in 2007. The goal of the four-year-project, still active as of this writing, funded by NSF, is to prepare a network of faculty with the skills to design, develop, and implement the PBCL process. ITL will improve and extend current PBCL practice by providing media-rich web-based and print materials developed by the partnership and disseminated via train-the-trainer strategy. The ITL project will disseminate best practices developed since the initial TEFATE project, even as new insights emerge.

The evolution of PBCL since 1998 demonstrates how a project matures through use. The TEFATE project asks, What's happening in the workplace? SEATEC asks the question, Can we create processes to emulate what happens in the workplace? The Case Files project asks the question, Can we systematically teach a process to allow faculty to create their own PBCL experiences? Finally, ITL explores the question, Can we disseminate the PBCL process online, as well as on site, in such a way that the process itself is embedded into how instruction flows and how content is determined in the context of the course?

The project names and terminology have changed, but the vision to reform technological educational has remained at the core. NSF must be credited for providing funding, allowing one phase to support another. Faculty involvement has been a key to success. PBCL has been adopted and adapted by over 400 faculty members from participating ATE programs in fourteen states across the nation, helping to form and encourage business partnerships with the educational process.

2

THE CASE FOR
PROBLEM-BASED CASE LEARNING

The PBCL approach enables educators to design learning based on problem solving, critical thinking, and current and authentic problematic situations encountered in business and industry. By bringing real-time, real-world problems to their students, instructors can significantly minimize the barriers that typically separate the classroom from the real world.

Fundamental Concepts of PBCL

The PBCL approach builds on more than three decades of research by leading experts in learning and cognition. In How People Learn, published by the National Research Council, John Bransford, Professor of Education at the University of Washington, synthesized three foundational principles of learning. PBCL is based on these principles:

Prior knowledge:

A critical part of approaching a problematic situation is to figure out what is already known about the situation at hand. People come to learning experiences with preconceptions. Our students come to class with various beliefs, experiences, and biases that affect how they learn. PBCL builds on the idea that learners construct new knowledge on what they already know. If their initial understanding is not engaged, they may not grasp new concepts or, even though they might "give back" information on a test, they may not be able to transfer that information to other activities outside the classroom.

Therefore, uncovering prior knowledge allows students to examine preconceptions and recognize misconceptions. Approaching prior knowledge with questioning and an investigative attitude preps the mind to think critically about the features of the situation.

PBCL experiences provide a rich backdrop to create a setting for understanding concepts, attitudes and skills.

Deep understanding:

Students need a background of factual information. PBCL incorporates the notion that the content of the course can be taught within the context of the problem. Learning concepts and skills within a meaningful context enables students to organize their learning in ways that facilitate retrieval and application.

Furthermore, individuals with their own perspectives can express these differences without losing the integrity of meaning in the process. This way understanding is gained through circumstances rather than by a step-by-step process done in lock step formation. The subtleties of nuance can be brought out depending on the situation.

Appreciation of differences creates a mosaic of thought rather than a lock-step movement just through a series of steps. Creativity of thought is an integrated part of thought, construction, and imagination. PBCL gives students new and diverse ways of thinking through a series of situations, a means of putting ideas together, or paths to proposed solutions. Depth of understanding increases as learners think together about the situation at hand and wonder where they can go next.

Metacognition:

PBCL depends on a metacognitive approach to instruction. Learning occurs when students reflect upon what they've done or think about what they have already processed and evaluated the efficacy of that thought. Reflection as an instructional strategy may be overlooked or eliminated in traditional classes because of time constraints, but with PBCL, reflection is an integral part of the learning process. "Thinking about thinking" is essential for reflective practice to develop.

These factors contribute to deep understanding of concepts and skills that promotes innovative thinking about what to do next. The ability to adapt to new situations, sometimes referred to as "adaptive expertise," is the hallmark of transfer, an indicator of "deep understanding."

Characteristics of PBCL

PBCL structures a learning experience around current, authentic problems from business or industry and employs proven learning techniques that are natural to the way people learn. Students learn technical content within the context of a problem. Learning comes from actually solving the problem.

Pilot testing in community colleges and universities has provided practitioners the opportunity to adapt and refine examples of PBCL. Some faculty integrate problem-based case learning experiences into existing classes, while others develop entire courses around PBCL, but these characteristics remain at the core of problem-based case learning:

Based upon authentic business problems.

Cases come from the "real world." Large corporations have collaborated with students on cases, but many business partners are small local companies. Students are engaged as "stakeholders" in the process of solving real problems. These are not contrived situations but ones found in the actual work place of today.

Sources for the situations can come from community associates, fellow teachers, business partners, fellow members of professional associations, friends and others. Getting started on a strong business problem is one of the most important steps to be made in developing a plan for students work a PBCL. Another source of business problems can be from the students' experience since many students will have business experience they can draw from.

Messy problems.

Students work in teams to define and work through messy, ill-defined problems. In fact, an important part of the process is defining what the problem really is. A great deal of emphasis is on working through all possibilities as problem solvers at this stage. Often when students seem to be stuck at this stage it relates to how the question or the situation is phrased. It lacks complicated issues, or issues with more than one possible response. The more the faculty can remain distanced from conversations with the student groups, letting students struggle, take notes, investigate, regroup, and formulate their ideas as a team, the better.

Teacher as facilitator.

Rather than acting as a "dispenser of knowledge," the instructor looks at how the students are learning, provides them with resources or with guidance to find resources when the time is right, and works with them to assess what they've learned. Far from just leaving students on their own, the teacher keeps a close eye on development of the teams' resources, questions, and tentative decisions in pursuit of their investigation.

Many groups often develop notebooks of findings in categories that track their research. Teachers can facilitate the beginning of this process by equipping students with a tool called the "Need to Know Board." This is an organizing board with four columns – Know, Assume, Question, and Resources. (See www.makinglearningreal.org)

The key behind this tool is to make visible what is known or assumed about the situation; to uncover what is "assumed" and to check that assumption; to surface questions relative to the issue in discussion; and to list resources needed for the answer to that particular question or in any other way needed. The group of students can work from the NKTB throughout the entire PBCL project.

Multiple solutions.

There is not one right answer or one right way of getting to an answer. Each team develops a solution based on the information they have collected. One of the strengths of the PBCL process is that students are able to construct multiple solutions to the question. The ability to discuss these possible solutions gives the students in the team a much broader perspective about the problem and its possible solutions.

Interdisciplinary.

PBCL integrates skills and knowledge from many areas. Students learn technical and business concepts and develop interpersonal skills as they propose solutions to the problematic situations they will encounter in the workplace. Academic skills, especially, are effectively integrated into the PBCL process. Students cannot solve the problem without communicating with other team members, with the business partner, the teacher, and possibly other students. Mathematics, communications, both written and oral, social sciences, library and research skills are all critical skills for the student to exercise while solving the PBCL problems.

PBCL serves as a curriculum organizer, toolkit, and instructional strategy to support the development of knowledge, skills, and attitudes needed in the workplace. Among the components of PBCL that instructors find valuable are resources for finding and collaborating with local business partners; guidelines for integrating problematic business situations into the curriculum; processes for establishing an effective structure for the learning experience; criteria for assessing student work and deliverables; and methods for instruction that support engaged student learning.

The Learning Cycle

Research findings present instructors with a conundrum. Because of the highly structured, instructor-focused nature of traditional learning environments, students may fail to acquire the knowledge, skills, and attitudes required in today's workforce. On the other hand, because of the lack of structure in non-traditional, student-focused learning environments, students may fail to acquire the knowledge, skills and attitudes assessed in most educational settings.

The PBCL Cycle is designed to resolve this conflict. Its stages describe the structure and process through which instructors, students, and business partners navigate each PBCL experience.

Researchers have concluded that problem-based, open-ended problems that arise from actual business situations produce powerful learning outcomes for students. PBCL provides a win/win/win situation for students, faculty, and business.

Figure 3:
The Stages of the PBCL Cycle

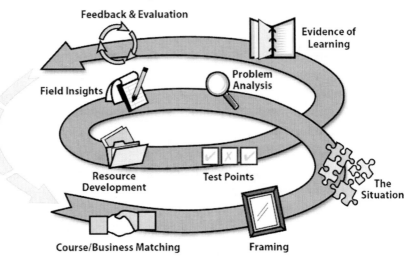

There are nine stages to the Learning Cycle:

The following paragraphs define the stages of the cycle and explain what should occur at each point.

1. Course/Business Matching:

The cycle begins when the link is established between the curriculum and the local business partner providing the problematic situation. In this initial stage, the instructor and business partner work together to accomplish these objectives:

- evaluate if and where course concepts and skills are visible in the business partner's workplace
- identify and analyze authentic contexts in which these concepts and skills are relevant to addressing problematic situations currently affecting the business partner
- determine where in the curriculum the problematic situations should form the context for learning.

2. Framing:

When the problematic situation has been selected and positioned within the course, the business partner and instructor continue to make these important decisions:

- determine student deliverables that will be used to provide evidence of learning
- define criteria and methods that will be used to assess and evaluate the students' performance
- develop a plan for effective collaboration that will establish clear roles and responsibilities for the instructor and business partner
- identify necessary support and tools for completing the project.

It is important to note that the task of actually defining the problem is left for the student teams in the next steps of the Learning Cycle.

3. The Situation:

In this stage, students are introduced to the problematic situation and the PBCL Cycle. The instructor, possibly together with the business partner, is responsible for the following:

- presents the problematic situation in context using multiple perspectives, a variety of media, and the minimum amount of information necessary to form a foundation of understanding
- reviews the PBCL process and the PBCL Cycle through which the students, instructor, and business partner will work together
- invites the students to initiate their role as active, responsible learners by encouraging them to ask questions and to extend their thinking about the problematic situation.

4. Problem Analysis:

Each team of students must form a hypothesis to uncover the problem embedded in the situation. This stage of the PBCL Cycle is structured so the teams of students accomplish the following:

- use a variety of tools and questioning techniques to identify and evaluate facts, assumptions, questions to ask, and resources needed to research options
- negotiate priorities, decision-making criteria, and the formation of hypotheses
- explore and begin building skills in collaborative teamwork and reflective learning.

5. Field Insights:

After each team of students has identified a problem to address, their goal is to achieve a deep understanding of the particular problem as they see it. To accomplish this, students will work together on the following:

- review primary source documents, internet sites and search results, and content-related periodicals and books
- conduct interviews of business partners and relevant industry experts via on-site visits or conference calls
- use a variety of tools and techniques to organize information, share insights, and integrate the analysis of data from multiple sources.

6. Resource Development:

As in the business world, research has to stop at some point. This stage of the PBCL Cycle is structured so that each team of students completes its research when the team has enough information to begin proposing solutions. Student teams will address the following:

- identify gaps and make plans to address missing information or perspectives
- execute any revisions needed to ensure that the team's information is accurate and relevant
- form hypotheses about solutions to the problematic situation.

7. Test Points:

At this point, students are ready to make decisions and prepare to back them up. Each team will go through these steps:

- perform a final check of the significance and validity of information and information sources
- decide what solution or solutions to propose
- review and evaluates the process by which they reached their solution(s)
- develop strategies for selecting, consolidating and presenting information to support the team's proposed solution(s)
- create the presentation, relevant media and support materials
- consider how the approach to identifying a problem and developing solution(s) demonstrates the significance of course-related concepts.

8. Evidence of Learning:

With business partner, instructor, and fellow students as their audience, student teams are ready to show their work, with these final steps:

- present the problem they have identified and the related solution(s)
- explain the reasoning behind their identified problem and solution(s)
- encourage audience inquiry and invites feedback.

9. Feedback and Evaluation:

The instructor facilities a discussion during which all the participants – instructor, business partner, and students – can accomplish certain objectives:

- determine if revisions are necessary to each team's problem description and proposed solution(s)
- evaluate individual and team performance; reflect on learning

achieved by students, instructors, and business partners and on the PBCL process
- celebrate the students' success.

Instructors and business partners will also take the opportunity for further evaluation and planning, with these steps:

- evaluate which, if any, of the proposed solutions might be implemented by the business partner to address the problematic situation
- determine how the instructor and students might be involved in the solution's implementation
- recommend changes to course content and instructional approaches
- plan their ongoing partnership and prepare for the selection of future problematic situations
- reflect on the value contributed by and distributed among the students, instructor, and business partner.

The design of the PBCL Cycle demonstrates the importance of structure, without sacrificing the flexibility needed for PBCL which supports an approach to learning based on inquiry. In fact, by encouraging students to return to previous states – to revisit ideas, information, conclusions, evidence or plans for moving forward – the looping structure of the PBCL Cycle is also an accurate representation of learning in the real world.

The PBCL cycle illustrates how important a partnership is to the learning process. It all begins with the teacher and business partner discussing and selecting a business situation that best illustrates the concepts to be presented and learned by the students. The involvement of the business partner assures that the problem students will face is a current, realistic, multifaceted, and authentic business problem. In the ideal situation, the business partner presents the problem to the students in such a way that they feel their efforts will be precisely like they will face when employed later in their career.

The students must learn that solving a "real business problem" is complex and consists of interpersonal skills, communications skills, investigation skills, and technical skills that integrate all aspects of the problem. The business partner participates as appropriate with students, answering questions and giving a broader perspective of the problem if asked to. Teachers typically do not "give out" information but help direct students to appropriate resources that will help them understand and work toward a solution. The teacher's role is to coordinate the learning process and to encourage all students to participate in the solution to the problem. The business partner listens to the reports from each of the student groups and again provides feedback, encouragement and information as necessary. As evidenced by comments made by several business partners, this involvement has provided them with an opportunity to "know" the students and to identify students with particular skills that they would like to employ after graduation.

How Is PBCL Different from Traditional Instruction?

Problem-based case learning builds upon pre-existing instructional methodologies, with which it shares many features. A significant similarity is that students are actively engaged in creating their own collaborative learning experiences. Another similarity is that concepts and skills are learned within the context of their real-world applications. Working in teams is also part of methodologies, such as project-based learning.

Considerable research suggests that these features are necessary but not sufficient for improved student learning. So to help students more fully achieve the potential of earlier instructional methodologies, the PBCL approach includes a "real-time" problematic business situation and a structural framework, the Learning Cycle, upon which instructors can build their curricula.

The "real-time" aspect of the PBCL approach heightens the recognition that there are no pre-determined "correct" answers in most authentic business scenarios, but rather messy situations with multiple perspectives on the issues. It also increases the motivation and engagement of all stakeholders since the learners have the potential to have an observable and measurable impact on the business.

Bringing real-world context to course content benefits learners and offers a "check-and-balance" to content in a rapidly changing technological world. For example, the CAD class had been using a common computer program to teach the concepts of CAD. However, in the last few years it has become increasingly difficult to find businesses that are using that program. Because of the PBCL process where instructors work with individuals from several businesses, they have learned that other programs are more common today. Therefore, the CAD department has expanded their course offerings, using PBCL techniques, to include other types of CAD programs.

The PBCL Cycle provides a clear road map for the learning process. Instructors using the PBCL Cycle ensure that students make consistent progress as they navigate the otherwise loosely structured learning experience. Unlike traditional case study methodologies, the PBCL approach begins with students clarifying the nature of the problem, rather than being "given the problem."

While there is value in the use of historical case studies, i.e. studying why the Challenger exploded, real-time situations provide a variety of additional benefits. No solutions have been implemented, so the situation is wide open for exploration. There is a level of importance and urgency that motivates all the participants, and students can interact with the business partner, whether to identify resources or refine their solution(s) to fit the situation.

PBCL encourages creative thinking by allowing the problem to be open-ended, fostering the development of several solutions to the problematic situation. It integrates technical concepts, teamwork, communications and interpersonal skills. Research findings have demonstrated that transfer of learning improves when students use the Learning Cycle.

3

PROBLEM-BASED CASE LEARNING IN ACTION

Insights from administrators, business partners, teacher-trainers, faculty, and students who have been involved with PBCL reveal how the business partnership works in the classrooms, how PBCL has affected student learning, and how it continues to transform technological education.

Administrative Perspective/Observations

Jim Johnson

When Jim Johnson arrived at Nashville State Community College for his first day as the Dean of Technology, he was informed that the college had just received word from the National Science Foundation that two grant proposals were going to be funded. Jim was asked to be the principal investigator for one of the grants, The Case Files, and to be in an advisory committee member for the other which was a grant for The Center for Information Technology Education (CITE).

The concept of Problem Based-Case Learning (PBCL) had been defined in an earlier project called SEATEC and was to be expanded in the two new grants. The Case Files was to use that concept, develop several examples of cases, and find ways to integrate them into the curriculum. At the same time CITE was concentrating on developing business relationships that would spawn new problem-based learning experiences to be incorporated in the technology courses at Nashville State and other cooperating schools and colleges.

"What an opportunity for a new Dean," Jim says, "to help faculty bring business partners into the classroom and help students understand the current problems in businesses and how to apply their course work to help solve those problems." However, Jim recalls that "my naiveté caused me to overlook many of the 'everyday' situations, requirements and administrative challenges that would resist widespread implementation of PBCL."

The first challenge was to help faculty see the importance of using PBCL in their classes. "What's wrong with the way we're currently teaching?" was a common reaction from teachers who were asked to consider using PBCL. "I already use business applications in my class" was another common reaction from teachers. In some cases that was true, but in far too many cases, Jim says, topics were being taught the same way as they were several years ago, even though the technology had changed.

He was also reminded by faculty that they had an Industrial Advisory Committee that met periodically to evaluate and give recommendations concerning the curriculum. Because Industrial Advisory Committees were required by the state, committee meetings were typically held twice each year for each technology department. Jim describes how the meetings would often go: "Two to four industrial advisors would attend. These were frequently 'friends of the program' or of the faculty members. After introductory small talk usually related to last week's Tennessee Titans football game, lunch was served along with more small talk. Now that a large portion of the meeting time had been consumed, the agenda was presented. It included topics currently of interest to the faculty such as enrollment statistics, graduation rates, placement data, and occasionally a discussion on curriculum topics. After the meeting, the advisors were thanked and invited to come next time, minutes of the meeting were written and placed in the file, and the file drawer closed. Only rarely was the question proposed: 'Are we teaching the necessary topics in a way that our students will be prepared for employment when they finish their program?'"

That was a question that needed to be asked. Teachers needed to be asking: "How can I be sure that what I'm teaching is important and necessary for my students to be prepared for employment?"

In PBCL this question is answered when the teacher and business partner work together to identify a "problem." This problem should be something recently encountered by the business partner. It should not be such a high-priority item that the business considers it "mission critical," but on the other hand, it should not be a problem so trivial that a solution would be of no interest to the business partner. In virtually any business, there are problems that fall between those two extremes.

Those problems in the middle classification would be of value to the business partner if the problem were solved but are not of such a priority that the business partner has time himself to work on a solution. The solution of this middle group of problems has enough value that the business partner will spend time helping the teacher and/or students understand the problem and to give counsel and advice. It is a real problem that the business partner may be able to incorporate in his process and thus the problem has significance to both the student and the business partner. This situation is a win-win-win opportunity. It is of value to the business partner; it is interesting and important to the student, and the teacher has an excellent opportunity to apply theoretical principles to an authentic problem.

Finding a business partner who is willing to identify and share problems of this type is not difficult, Jim believes, but it takes extra effort on the part of the teacher because he or she needs to initiate the process. The teacher must always be seeking that business partner.

The faculty member should be willing to network within professional organizations where potential business partners are likely to be. Professional societies covering virtually all technologies are active in nearly every community. Their members are usually very willing to work with educational programs to identify problems and to communicate with the instructor and students. Personal contacts are also important. Teachers frequently meet potential business partners in service organizations such as Kiwanis, Lions Clubs, computer user groups and even church groups.

"Nothing is more important to the success of PBCL than a teacher's willingness to be actively engaged with professionals in their teaching field," Jim notes. This personal commitment will not only provide good situations to be used in PBCL activities but it will help stimulate the program's advisory committee. These professionals need to hire well-prepared workers. The more the business partner is involved with the college's program and its students, the more the program will meet the business partner's expectations. Remember, this is a win-win-win proposition.

Jim recalls one of the first meetings with business partners, students and teachers. Several professional-looking business partners from a major U.S. manufacturing corporation attended the meeting to define and discuss the problem they were proposing. Students came to this first meeting in their usual informal attire, displaying an attitude of indifference. The business partners matter-of-factly defined the situation they wanted the students to work on and as they did, the students seemed astonished. "You want us to do that?" they asked.

The students worked on this problematic situation for most of the semester. The teacher worked with the students, serving as a resource guide and counselor to help them formulate potential solutions to the problem. At the end of the semester, the business partners came to campus for a second meeting to allow the students to present their solutions to the proposed problem. This time the students entered the meeting room in appropriate dress, neatly groomed, to make their presentations. Each four-member team presented different solutions. The business partners were pleased because now they had multiple potential solutions to consider. After this meeting it was the business partners who were impressed with the students' quality of work, interest in the situation, and professionalism of presentations.

Over several years, teachers have implemented PBCL differently in their classes, but in each case the focus is the relationship with business partners. Sometimes instructors use new problems defined by new business partners, but it is time consuming to develop multiple new cases each semester. To help overcome the burden of time, some instructors have recorded interviews with business partners from previous cases so they can present the same case again to a new group of students. Some of the personal contact is lost, but the students encounter the same intensity of problem solving and even recommend different solutions.

Also, in some technologies, it is virtually impossible to find project ideas that can be done by a few students in a few weeks. For instance, in Architecture Technology it is no surprise that the instructor has not been able to find architectural clients who are willing to turn over the design of multi-million dollar buildings to students. Therefore, he has formed a "campus planning committee" that consists of teachers and administrators from different areas of the college. That committee functions as a business partner and helps the students by defining virtual building projects on campus. It is well known that these buildings will not be built but the process defined by the committee adds realism to the project. The committee of volunteers has shown great interest in helping to provide this realistic environment for the students to work within.

However, involvement of business partners is critical to the success of PBCL. Ideally, a new business problem would be defined by a partner each semester for each class. This would include introductory classes as well as those in the middle of the program and capstone courses as the culminating part of a program. However, it is understood that it is nearly impossible for a new PBCL case to be developed and presented each semester and even more unrealistic when faculty members teach multiple courses. Techniques have been identified to produce essentially the same result. The following is a hierarchy of ways PBCL can be applied:

- Arrange for an actual business partner to present a real problem to students and teacher.
- Use a recording of an actual business partner presenting a real problem to students and teacher.
- Use prepared cases available at www.thecasefiles.org. Model cases that originated from business partners have been prepared for delivery via the web as examples.
- Simulate a business partner such as described above for Architectural Technology.

Here are ways of obtaining cases that do not make use of PBCL methodology:

- Using a teacher's own business experience. It is difficult for teachers to play the role of a business partner and the teacher. This technique has worked in limited cases where the teacher is an adjunct who is also employed as a business partner, but this method is not recommended.
- Using fictitious situations made up by the teacher.
- Using examples from the text book.

- Using problem assignments from the text book.

Jim notes that some classes lend themselves naturally to the use of PBCL. Upper level courses where students are preparing to enter the workforce are more obvious courses for PBCL implementation. The example presented in Chapter 4 of this book by Dale Rogers is an excellent example of using PBCL in a capstone course that has extensive business partner involvement.

However, to take that same concept and apply it to first or second semester students is a much greater challenge. Since the world of experiences may be limited for these students, it is more difficult (but not impossible) to find business problems that they can relate to. Frequently, introductory classes will have some students enrolled who are more experienced and can function as mentors for the other students. In no case should the instructor assume that a "real, business-oriented" problem is out of reach for the class. There are some very creative ways to bring real business problems into the classroom. For instance, when it is impossible to identify enough real business problems each semester, the instructor can adapt other prepared cases, such as cases designed in The Case Files project.

Jim gives an example: the Introduction to Engineering Technology course taught at Nashville State. Several years ago, each technology program had a course entitled "Introduction to _____ Technology." Each course was virtually the same and was taught by a faculty member from each specific discipline. When PBCL was introduced at Nashville State, a new introductory course was developed. All ET students were enrolled in the same course. Thus, students who were enrolled in Electrical, Electronic, Civil, Construction or Architectural Engineering Technology were classmates in their first course. PBCL was identified as the teaching technique to be used for all sections of these courses regardless of the instructors' field of technology or students' selected majors.

Instructors could choose from the model cases developed by The Case Files project and presented on the web site for use in this course, even though only about three cases could be completed in a specific semester. Students worked in teams to solve problems covering a wide range of technologies. The focus of the course was problem solving in teams and presentations to explain the results. A variety of strategies including teamwork, web search, computer programs, personal contacts with outside experts, and library research were used to help students solve their problem.

Jim explains how, in the Introduction to Engineering Technology course, the instructor would present useful topics such as the Excel program, and students would experience "educational side trips" as they realized that the use of the computer spreadsheet program Excel, including the graphing, would help them solve problems. The instructor would present short problems such as "graphically show the relationship between electrical current and voltage as voltage increases from 0 to 250 volts in a circuit of given resistance." The students could even be given Ohm's law because that was not the objective of the assignment; instead, the use of Excel to solve a graphics problem was the assignment. Students working together could complete this problem in one class period or less and would have developed the necessary skills to use the Excel program again in more advanced problems. Several short problem (side trips) assignments such as these helped students develop the skills and knowledge to use various tools to solve the larger, more complex PBCL problem.

Introduction to Engineering Technology and the Media Production classes were designed to be taught primarily using PBCL, and it is obvious that the business partner involvement is very different. In Media Production, actual business clients present a problem to be solved by student groups in virtually the same way these students will solve problems for clients after they graduate and are employed. In Introduction to Engineering Technology the real business partnership comes from video and audio reproductions of interviews with business partners. Due to the number of cases used each semester in Introduction to Engineering Technology it would be virtually impossible for the instructor to identify all new cases to use each semester, although we recommend that faculty be involved in development of at least one new case each semester, even at the introductory level.

Jim explains that other courses have not been able to adjust their curriculum outlines so that PBCL drives instruction. These teachers use at least one case in their class that may take several days to several weeks to complete. Using cases in classes with existing course outlines is difficult in many ways. First, students need to become oriented to the problem-based case learning approach. Using PBCL for only a few weeks (or days) out of a semester requires that students change their approach to processing and learning during the semester. "This frequently puts the student at a disadvantage and often wastes time for both the teacher and the student," Jim says.

Secondly, PBCL courses integrate topics in a way similar to the way they are used in business. Teacher-led courses structure content material in an outline or other organized way in an attempt for students to build one topic upon the completion of another topic in a serial way. This may be an effective way to organize and present material for a classroom experience, but it is not the way the students will apply the information when they move to a work environment. How will students learn to apply the topics to a work environment if they have learned them only in a sequenced, traditional way? Employers report that students who have been exposed to PBCL have a much shorter learning curve after they start their first employment than do students who have studied the same material in a traditional format. Use of PBCL in any amount in any class will help students prepare for employment, but best results have been found when the curriculum of an entire course is adapted to use PBCL strategies through a clear rationale.

Another challenge to implementing PBCL has occurred when several sections of the same class are taught by different instructors. For instance, in an introductory math class where six sections are taught by three instructors, each teaches two sections. If the teachers do not agree to use the same teaching technique, problems can occur.

Jim recalls an illustration of this that occurred at NSCC when a math teacher used PBCL, working with a local business, to teach graphical analysis. This teacher had four sections; two used PBCL and two used traditional teaching techniques. Other teachers were teaching sections of the same math course also using traditional methods. Data taken by the math teacher indicated that the students using the PBCL approach learned the graphical information as well as the traditional students but were much better prepared to transfer their knowledge to new graphical problems than were traditional students.

The PBCL students enjoyed the course much more and were

interested in the topic, which was not evident with the students in the traditional math classrooms. However, after one semester of trial and measurement in two classes, the other instructors decided all courses must cover the same topics in the same way and PBCL was "outvoted" by the department.

As the Dean of Technology and Principal Investigator for the NSF-sponsored projects, Jim Johnson was able to observe several interesting characteristics about PBCL and its applications in various classes. He believes the success factors for PBCL include both the instructor and administrative support. Without exception, the most successful PBCL teachers are those that have had business-related experience prior to entering their teaching career. Due to previous experience, they were more inclined to comprehend the business partner's situation, his environment, and the urgency of solving the problem. Business-experienced teachers find it easier to identify the most realistic and logical problem to be attempted. They can also help the business partner express his thoughts properly and at the right level for students to understand. The business-experienced teacher can see the advantage and importance of the business relationship, which is critical to the success of PBCL.

"Administrative support is critical for several reasons," Jim points out. He recalls that many times students came to his office to complain that a teacher was not providing the information needed to solve a problem or that the material was not in the textbook or that the teacher did not 'explain' something but sent them to another resource. "I attempted to explain to the students why the teacher was not lecturing or not following the text book exactly," Jim says, "and relate that directly to employment after college." Students typically accepted that explanation, but Jim also notes that when it came time for them to evaluate the teacher at the end of the semester, the students expressed their feelings again.

"Virtually, all teachers in my division received lower student ratings as a result of implementing PBCL," he says. "The teachers were still doing an excellent job but students did not understand why the teacher was taking a 'non-conventional' teaching approach." Jim was able to follow some of those students after they graduated and started employment, however, and they had already begun to see the advantage of the teaching technique used by that teacher. "Only then did they realize that the instructor was really doing an exceptional teaching job," Jim says.

Some of the experiences related to PBCL shared by faculty at NSCC and other colleges over the past ten years indicate that it is an exceptional teaching technique. It is much easier and more meaningfully applied to some technical topics than to others, but with some creativity on the part of the teacher and some support from administration and business partners, PBCL can be an effective strategy to use in virtually any technology classroom.

Jim notes that in every PBCL trial we can say with assurance that:

- Students learned the material as well or better using PBCL techniques than by using traditional teaching methods.
- Students who used PBCL were able to apply the material more effectively to real situations than students who were not exposed to PBCL techniques.
- Employers have reported that students involved with PBCL techniques in at least some classes were better equipped to start a new job. Their learning curve was shortened and students had a better understanding of how to function successfully in the work environment.
- Students developed methods of using outside resources to help them solve problem.
- Stronger and more useful relationships were developed between business partners and teachers which tended to improve program advisory committees.
- Students' initial response is that the teacher "is not teaching." Students are not accustomed to working on PBCL type problems and think the teacher is not doing everything he or she should.
- Administrative support is critical to support the teacher applying PBCL concepts in their course.
- In-service training is extremely important. Experienced PBCL teachers need to help newly employed teachers understand the PBCL concept and how to apply it. Teacher turnover is such that continual in-service training on PBCL is necessary.

Business Partner's Perspective/Observations

The business partner is the key to successful implementation of a PBCL experience. A working relationship and one of respect between the teacher and business partner are essential. Relationships with business partners need to be developed and cultivated continually because of the mobility of the business and educational staff. The example of a business partnership described below with Chris Beck is an excellent model to follow. Even though the Saturn Corporation was terminated by General Motors a few months ago, and the fact that EDS (Chris's employer when the case file was written) have both changed, the relationship between Nashville State and Chris has continued to evolve.

Chris Beck

Chris Beck first became a business partner with Nashville State classes while he was an account manager at Electronic Data Systems (EDS), an IT consulting firm located at the Saturn Manufacturing Campus in Spring Hill, TN. EDS was a supporter of Nashville State, participating in other school initiatives, so the classroom involvement was a natural evolution of that existing relationship.

Chris worked with students and instructors on several business problems, but one stands out to him. Chris brought a real-time situation into the classroom, challenging student teams to help define a new solution that would enable field operations consultants for Saturn to communicate effectively with the corporation when they were out visiting the retail partners at the Saturn automobile dealerships. Chris made several visits to the classroom and arranged for students to visit the business, as well. Throughout the semester, he communicated with the teams via e-mail and telephone conference calls. At the end of the semester, he attended the presentations by the teams. Five teams gave presentations, each with a different solution. Chris was impressed by students' professional manner and by the fresh set of creative ideas that they brought to help solve the business problem.

Chris's responsiveness and engagement with students might not be typical of every business partner, but he notes that his involvement "was reasonably easy to fit into the schedule. It took time and commitment, but not an enormous amount." He says he chose to work with the classes to give back to the community and help prepare more individuals for the IT profession. He points to the fact that there is a shortage of workers in the IT profession, and his participation with classes was a good way to help prepare future IT professionals.

From the point of view of a business leader, Chris has some thoughts about how college classes should be preparing students for the workplace. "In the IT profession, I believe we need to be teaching our students business skills in addition to technical skills," he says. "These skills are even more important during difficult economic times when proper business assessments need to be done to determine the best solution to a business problem." He points out that problem-solving is at the heart of what IT professionals do. Also, Chris says it is critical for new IT professionals to be "adaptable, nimble, and have outstanding communication skills" because they will be interacting not only with customers but with peers who may be in locations around the globe.

Chris believes students who have been exposed to problem-based case learning are absolutely better prepared for the workplace. He says, "The ability to see, hear, and work in a business environment and solve IT problems as part of a learning experience will better prepare our future IT professionals." His participation as a business partner has convinced him that through PBCL, "students engage more deeply, and as a result of that engagement, learn more." He believes that "the contextual learning models help students understand why and how what they are learning will be put to use." Finally, Chris says, "For those students that have not been exposed to the business world, [PBCL] provides a safe learning environment to help them understand how customers' and future clients' expectations are managed."

Instructors' Perspectives/Observations

The instructors represented below are good examples of different but creative ways that PBCL has been successfully implemented. In most cases, PBCL is used exclusively as the teaching technique in one (sometimes more) classes. Some of the following are illustrations of PBCL being used as the first course in a curriculum, as illustrated by Innocent Usoh's example.

PBCL has also been effective when used as the learning method for a capstone course as illustrated by the example of Dale Rogers. Other examples fall in between the first course and the last course in a curriculum. Each of the illustrations selected represents a unique way in which a teacher has incorporated PBCL in a class.

Susan Jones

Susan Jones's experience with The Case Files demonstrated that problem-based case learning is effective not only in advanced courses, but also in classes where students do not already have a solid foundation in the content. Susan developed a case for a developmental math course, and she and an adjunct instructor taught classes that represented control and experimental groups. The purpose of the case was to help students develop an understanding of proportional relationships, lines, equations of lines, and linear functions. *Understanding* was the key; students traditionally learned to plug numbers into the point-slope and slope-intercept forms of a line, without any contextual understanding of what the quantities represented.

The business partner was a large financial services corporation. The connection with the company came through a graduate course in statistics that Susan was teaching at a local university. One of her graduate students was interested in problem-based case learning and agreed to ask her employer for permission to work with Susan on an authentic business problem. The company provided survey data which related to customer satisfaction, which Susan modified for confidentiality purposes. Students used the mock data to make suggestions about where to allocate funds to increase and predict future revenues.

The developmental classes in intermediate algebra were made up of students who were unprepared for true college math. For some, high school was several years ago, and they had forgotten a lot of the math they once knew. Others never developed adequate skills in algebra.

Students in Susan's experimental group complained at first when the situation was introduced through a series of videos that set up the business situation. They "just wanted to do math." Problem-based case learning made them uncomfortable, especially the teamwork concept and the idea that there was *not one right answer*. Their complaints at the beginning contrasted with later comments, when many of the students began to see for the first time that math actually has real-world applications.

For a math instructor, building a course around PBCL was hard work and somewhat uncomfortable. Susan had some prior experience with groups in graduate courses, which worked to her advantage, but she says, "I had to grow, too." Over the next few semesters, as she gained experience with PBCL strategies and tools, she could anticipate stumbling blocks and prepare her students. As she saw the outcome of the experimental classes, she was able to alleviate some of the students' concerns in the beginning of the course about the effectiveness of working a real-world case to learn math concepts. She became more comfortable with the idea that she, as the teacher, didn't have to provide all the answers. "They came up with some solutions I hadn't thought of," Susan said.

Though the grades from the control and experimental classes were similar, Susan identified a dramatic difference in the traditional approach and the PBCL approach for teaching these concepts when students began to review for the final exam. Those who had worked the case demonstrated that they actually *understood* the mathematical concepts because they had applied those concepts in a real-world situation. The students in the control group relied on memorization, which was possible at that level, but left concerns about retaining the material beyond the end of the semester.

Jack Wallace

Jack Wallace has taught in the Architectural/Engineering Technology program at NSCC for three years, after a career in the private sector as a registered architect. Having worked on everything from small residential projects to multi-million-dollar corporate projects, Jack tries in all of his classes to make the problems as authentic as possible. He describes his approach to PBCL as "hybrid" because the process does not begin with an actual business representative coming to the class with a problem to solve. Jack does not expect any company to let students design its $30 million building, but he has found ways to get around that obstacle and still give his students the connection with business partners.

He has formed what he calls a Campus Planning Board, made up of faculty, staff, and members of the architectural advisory board, which includes architects and others from business and industry. The Campus Planning Board acts as the client – the business partner.

Jack uses NSCC's "Campus Master Plan" as a basis for projects for his Architectural Design Process class. Each semester, the class designs a different building. So far, his classes have developed a conference center, a wellness center, and a building for the police science program. These projects cover the entire semester, and Jack intersperses smaller-scale projects such as an outdoor classroom to teach specific concepts. He can draw from this inventory of projects for future classes, as well. A new "client" next semester, the new members that form the Campus Planning Board, will push the same building in a new direction.

Students in the architectural, civil, and construction engineering technology program at NSCC can participate in the national organization, ACESA, the Architectural and Civil Engineering Technology Student Association. Jack established the campus chapter to further introduce real-world ideas about architecture and engineering. The students organize field trips and lectures by visiting professionals, participate in community service, and learn about the professional organizations that are available in their fields.

One of the architects who designed the Schermerhorn Symphony Center, home to the Nashville Symphony, spoke at one of the meetings about acoustics design. Students have the opportunity to chat with working architects and engineers over pizza, and through the ACESA meetings, Jack has made business connections that are vital for his classes.

Several of the students in the Architectural Design Process course are changing careers; some are working toward a CAD certificate. The authentic problems introduced in the course engage the students and help prepare them for the architectural or engineering workplace. Jack has brought in architects to lead the student teams in basic design. He explains that most schools of architecture use a problem-based approach that is similar to PBCL, but PBCL takes it another positive step by making the project *realistic*. In architectural schools, the project theoretically has an unlimited budget. The jury that critiques the student work is made up of faculty members, who are architects, and the project is judged on the basis of concept and appearance. Jack points out that in the real world, an unlimited budget is rare, and the client is not the professor.

Partnering with the Campus Planning Board has been exciting because of how the group influences the direction of the project. One semester, the board rejected the students' initial designs, requiring the teams to reframe the problem. The authentic learning experience allows students to develop content knowledge, along with the skills and attitudes necessary for success in the real world.

John Magill

John Magill, who teaches courses in the Computer Information Technology program at Iowa Western Community College, has long been a proponent of experiential learning. When he was introduced to PBCL methodology through an "awareness workshop," he was looking for something different for his Introduction to Information Technology course. "It was the right time," he says. "PBCL struck a chord." After that, he used PBCL in the Intro course every semester that he taught the class. The course continues to be taught with PBCL by another instructor.

The course is organized around six or seven cases, using problematic situations from a retail business. The business contact, a member of their advisory board, is the corporate IT officer for a half-price retail company.

Cases involve software, hardware, networking, and logic problems, built around situations at one of the retail shops. John determines in the beginning the skills and concepts that he wants students to learn. Students break themselves up into teams and divide responsibilities. Though they don't work directly with the manager of the retail shop, "I always preface the case *as if* we're dealing with the manager," says John. Students take field trips to the corporate headquarters and talk with the corporate IT officer, who is able to provide information and answer questions during the semester.

PBCL energized the Intro class. The students, primarily recent high school graduates, "took hold of it," John says. He teaches classes in Linux, Windows, security, hardware repair, Cisco networking, and web programming. "We can tell a difference in later classes," he says. Students are more effective team members, having experienced PBCL concepts. They understand the process and look at problems in a different way. "PBCL has raised our cognitive training to a higher level," John notes.

He says that the students "have the benefit of how we've changed the curriculum and how we as teachers have changed." At Iowa Western, there are four full-time faculty, two regular part-time instructors, and a number of adjuncts. Though the Intro class is the only one that is "strictly PBCL," all of the instructors use PBCL concepts in some shape or form. "They don't expect students just to 'give back' answers," John says. In his other courses, he uses many of the PBCL components and tools such as the Need-to-Know Board. He has increased his use of teamwork. The current teacher of the Intro course is working with a new business partner to frame situations for the class.

"PBCL has helped us to enhance our advisory committee and increased our relationships with business partners," John says. He feels the school's reputation has been enhanced, resulting in more interest from businesses in working with the school and looking to hire their graduates.

Ted Kraus

Ted Kraus, an adjunct instructor in his third year at Nashville State Community College, teaches a variety of CAD classes and has developed the curriculum for two courses that use the software known as REVIT, a 3D building information management (BIM) modeler designed for use in the architectural field.

Initially, Ted used a traditional lecture-based teaching approach, but after a couple of semesters, he observed problem-based case learning (PBCL) strategies in some of his colleagues' classes and became involved in the Innovation in Teaching and Learning (ITL) project. He also began to understand how PBCL interfaced with the graduate work he had done in critical thinking and metacognition. As a result, he developed and implemented a curriculum based on PBCL for his advanced REVIT class.

Ted introduced a business partner to his class the first day. He had met Eric Klotz, an architect whose firm already had a relationship with NSCC's architecture department. Eric's proficiency in the use of REVIT made him a valuable resource, and he was willing to work with Ted on an unsolved problem for the class.

Ted handed out packets with information about the project that would be at the heart of the students' PBCL experience. Eric explained to the class that they were looking at a proposal for a job that had not moved forward. It was the perfect PBCL project in that it represented a problem that had not yet been solved, and it served to provide a contextual backdrop for framing the lectures Ted would give over the next few weeks.

After the students looked over the information packets, Ted asked them what they would need to know in order to successfully complete the project. Eric had helped Ted develop the syllabus, and the perspective of a working architect was evident in the syllabus. The students' ideas about what they would need to know were largely represented in the topics to be covered.

For the next seven weeks, Ted incorporated lab assignments into the class that not only reinforced the lectures but also produced work students would use in their final projects. During that time, Eric came back as a guest lecturer, and Ted was impressed by the level of discourse students had with Eric during his visits.

Groups for the final project were randomly chosen, and group members became responsible for organizing, scheduling, and monitoring the work. The class as a whole developed the rubric used for assessment, and the teams evaluated themselves. The students were excited about working with a business partner with a real problem to be solved, but at times they were frustrated by the fact that there was not a "right answer." Ted always tried to keep the focus on the process: *How do you make the decision?*

At the end of the semester, Eric, the business partner, returned for the presentations by three teams. Most of the students said they got more out of the class during the five-week final project than during the earlier part of the semester, and they wished they had started sooner. Ted is considering how he might structure the class to give them more time, asking himself: *What four or five things do they need to know right up front?* He is investigating how to integrate PBCL even more. He believes that as he gets more comfortable with the PBCL methodology, he can also integrate PBCL into the curriculum for the beginning REVIT class.

Ted has seen obvious benefits in implementing PBCL in his class. Many of the students in the advanced REVIT class are already out in the workplace; some would like to change jobs. The authenticity of PBCL is appealing. As Ted expressed it, "PBCL forces you to explore your knowledge base as you define your learning goals."

Melanie Butterbaugh

Melanie Butterbaugh teaches in computer science courses at Iowa Western Community College. New to PBCL, she is enthusiastic about how her teaching has changed since she has been implementing PBCL concepts.

It's fun to see "the spontaneity, the creativity, the different directions that they go that aren't anticipated," she says. "You just cannot imagine where they'll take you, and that is one of the best things about the course."

Melanie says that she would "absolutely" advise any other teacher to try PBCL. She admits it was hard to let go, to give up some of the control of what goes on in the class. "The format was difficult," she says. "I was not a facilitator; I was mostly a lecturer, the fountain of knowledge. I'm detail-oriented, so I needed to know what was going on, where they were headed, what were their thoughts." But now that she is comfortable using PBCL in her classroom, she says, "Teaching is what it was when I first started."

Beverly Bradley

A few years ago, Beverly Bradley was teaching courses in Program Logic and Design at NSCC when she was introduced to problem-based case learning. With her background as a mainframe computer programmer, she taught her course the way she had been taught - lecture and lab. The students in her four-hour night classes were bored. Each night she left class exhausted and discouraged that the students didn't seem to be learning. "I decided teaching was not for me. It was just too hard," Beverly recalls.

Then she took advantage of the opportunity to work on The Case Files, and the door to a whole new approach to teaching opened for her. "Problem-based case learning changed the way I taught and changed me," Beverly says. "I quit feeling guilty about not talking for four hours when I realized the value of having the students discover and present information themselves." As she began to use real-world situations and let students research, work in teams, and come up with their own solutions, teaching became fun. Beverly saw her students become more serious about learning the material when they had to apply it in a meaningful way.

In one of her first experiences with The Case Files, she used a case in her introductory class that was used previously in an advanced class. Though she realized that her students did not have the background to work the entire case, she introduced pieces of the case by teaching the content first - the more traditional approach - and then related pieces of the case to the content. Beverly felt it was a big accomplishment to modify her teaching approach in that way. She had learned that just as students arrive at multiple solutions to a given problem, so should teachers of PBCL realize that there were many ways to incorporate PBCL strategies into a given course. In another early case, the business partner who was supposed to supply certain information didn't come through, and Beverly learned another important lesson: Make sure in the beginning that the teacher and business partner understand how the course can benefit both the class and the business.

Beverly has taught a variety of courses since that time, using the business connection, teamwork, the process of discovery, and tools like the Need-to-Know Board. In a recent web design class, four teams worked with Feline Hotline, a local non-profit organization that finds adoptive homes for cats. Four student teams designed a website for the organization.

When the business partner initially met with the teams, the students "didn't know anything," Beverly recalls. She required them to keep weekly logs in which they recorded "what they wanted to happen and what really happened." The idea of grading themselves and their own team "freaked them out." In the end, two of the teams that presented their proposed websites to the business partners demonstrated excellent work. Another team came up with an acceptable but not superior website. The fourth team had one team member who didn't cooperate, and though Beverly discussed with team members how to handle the situation, they couldn't seem to get over that hurdle. While their web site was seriously incomplete, the students presented what they had accomplished to date. Even though they struggled, Beverly is confident that the process itself was a valuable learning experience for them.

She is learning, as well, how much to let teams struggle before she intervenes. She also stresses that the business partners must understand that they may receive a great solution or the project might crash and burn. Fortunately, in this case, the partner was delighted with the web sites presented.

Whether Beverly is teaching a course in computer information systems, web development, project management, or music technology, she embraces the concept of PBCL and finds ways to incorporate the strategies that have become part of her repertoire. Teaching continues to be fun, and it is most fun when students say, "I had no idea I could do this!"

Innocent Usoh

Engineering Technology 1000: Introduction to Engineering Technology, taught by Innocent Usoh, was one of the first courses at NSCC to be structured around problem-based case learning. From beginning to end, students work several cases that introduce engineering concepts and help them make the transition from high-school to business-related courses.

The Engineering Technology 1000 class is usually populated by students who have been away from an academic environment for a while. They have come back to re-train for a career in one of the engineering disciplines. Before this course was developed, many of the students who desired to go into the ET program but whose math skills were deficient gave up on college before ever getting far enough to take courses in their major. The remedial math requirement was too discouraging.

Engineering Technology 1000 does not require a mathematics pre-requisite. Built around PBCL methodology, the foundational course introduces students to various aspects of engineering and helps develop the skills, knowledge, and attitudes that students need for success in the engineering disciplines. After taking the introductory course, students are better prepared to tackle college math and the other courses in their major.

Innocent Usoh uses the cases that were originally created as part of The Case Files. After some introductory material that focuses on basic computer programs, geometry review, and research, Innocent moves the class quickly into teamwork. Some students may initially resist the "team" process, but when they begin working on the first case, they start to see that each individual can bring something valuable to the process. One may know Power Point or Excel; another may be an effective writer, while another may have good organizational skills. Students begin to gain confidence in their abilities.

The four or five cases introduced during the semester represent several engineering disciplines and parallel the situations that occur in the field. Initially, when the cases were developed, a business partner actually provided the unsolved problem, served as a resource as students worked through the problem, and attended class when the teams made their presentations. The scenarios and the PBCL tools have been duplicated to accurately represent real cases. The business partner is central to the PBCL experience; The Case Files developed an inventory of cases to help bring the PBCL process into the classroom when it is not feasible to work with an actual business partner. Through video clips, students in the intro course who work from the inventory of recycled cases can experience a version of the original business connection.

Innocent has seen the benefits of PBCL as students improve in areas of leadership, critical thinking, creativity, interpersonal relations, planning and problem-solving. Because he also teaches other courses in the engineering program, he knows that PBCL is changing students' thought processes as they embrace the concepts of a business-oriented environment. Engineering Technology 1000 demonstrates that PBCL works in introductory courses, where a real-time problematic situation is the hallmark of the experience.

Students' Perspectives/Observations

The real proof of any curriculum design or teaching method lies in the success of the students as they enroll in other courses or as they become employed. Employers have stated that recent graduates who have had one or more courses where PBCL was the primary teaching technique have a faster learning curve when they start a new job. Their ability to see the "complete picture" of the assignment and the ability to integrate various topics to come up with a possible solution are greatly enhanced for PBCL students. The employers have also commented that the PBCL students' ability to communicate and apply mathematical principles is greatly enhanced. The following is a selection of interviews with students who learned the PBCL method in college and are now employed.

David Calloway, Jr.

A student at Iowa Western Community College, David Calloway, Jr. was accustomed to classes in which the instructors came up with assignments and used the assignments over and over in every class, year after year. PBCL was an exciting new concept, offering the opportunity for students to be "more hands-on" in their classes. He describes it as "fresh." He says, "You feel like you're more needed in the classroom."

Lisa Gonser

Lisa Gonser has a business degree and a rewarding job in the corporate world, but her dream is to design houses. Her courses at NSCC have helped to prepare her for a career in residential design, and she is especially grateful that she has experienced problem-based case learning strategies in CAD, building codes, design, and presentation classes - all revolving around a real problem to solve.

In Jack Wallace's Architectural Design Process course, Lisa was a member of one of the teams that designed a wellness center. Jack gave some basic information about the project, and then students met with the Campus Planning Board to work on a needs analysis. Lisa remembers the students' reaction when they began to frame the problem and understood the magnitude of the project: *Wow! Can we do all of this?* Then Jack brought in architects from firms in Nashville to work with the teams during the initial design phase. The students were off and running. They studied existing site plans and looked up zoning regulations. They took the project from the needs analysis through design, drawings, models, to presentation. The architects who had worked with the students at the beginning of the semester returned for the final class and provided feedback on the team presentations.

"All the students thoroughly enjoyed the involvement of the architects," Lisa says. The teamwork aspect was another important real-world application, Lisa knows from her experience in the corporate world. "You always have slackers, and you always have team members who work harder than everyone else."

Lisa has carried problem-based case learning into her present job by incorporating real-world projects whenever her team members participate in a training class. She explains, "In a recent management training class, we substituted some of our current financial goals for the items in the stock training material and then applied the problem-solving tools we were learning in the class. We came up with some great ideas." A training class scheduled for the future will take current reports that are running in old software and let the trainees actually build the same reports in a new database that will allow them to access data as a cube as opposed to a flat file list.

Using problem-based case learning strategies in the classroom has two major benefits, according to Lisa: "It makes the time the students spend working on this useful and they grasp the tools more readily when they can incorporate information they already know."

Lisa summarizes her experience with PBCL by saying, "I think the key is that it makes you think on your own. You aren't just a parrot repeating what you are told; you are actually applying what you are learning. Reading something is one thing, but actually doing it takes it to another level. I can read about commercial building codes all day, but the challenge came when I actually had to help design a building and had to incorporate codes into the design. That was when I really saw the value."

G.K. Seeley

A recent graduate with his A.A.S. degree in the architectural/ engineering (A/E) program, G.K. Seeley has experienced problem-based case learning in several courses taught by Jack Wallace. While taking classes at NSCC, G.K. was also working part-time at a large A/E firm in Nashville. The PBCL situation and process he encountered in the Architectural Design Process class paralleled the projects that architectural teams designed and developed at the firm where he worked. Teamwork was a key component. Skills in communication, interpersonal relations, and problem-solving were valuable outcomes of the class. G.K. had observed these real-world skills in practice in the architectural workplace.

His class was given the task of designing a wellness center. The A/E firm where G.K. worked was one of the business partners participating in the Campus Planning Committee that Jack formed to help students determine what elements should be part of the building. G.K. was hoping to get hired full time after graduation. Architects from the firm were among those who attended the presentations at the end of the semester. "I was really nervous about presenting in front of my co-workers," G.K. says, "but it felt good. They were real architects asking real-life questions, which gave me a sense of some of the things to come in the future. They could have been any architects giving constructive criticism and trying to help." Did he get the job? Yes!

Now as a full-time draftsman, he recognizes more than ever the benefits of the PBCL experience. Every day he uses what he learned about problem-solving, communicating effectively, and working in teams. G.K. says he wouldn't change anything about Jack Wallace's class. He appreciated Jack's approach. "Jack didn't give us the answers. He would ask the question back, let you answer your own question," G.K. says.

Jessica Williams

Jessica Williams is a student on the A.A.S. degree track. She would like to go on to architectural school at a university after she leaves NSCC, and she plans to take other courses here that let her experience problem-based case learning, like the recent advanced REVIT class. She notes that she took both REVIT classes, both taught by Ted Kraus, but she is most excited about the advanced class.

"We learned teamwork, communication, and problem solving," she explains. She points out the value of "having to make it work," and the fact that Ted was "more interested in the process than the end result" brought about a new way of looking at problems. "He'd ask, 'Why did you do it that way? What was your reasoning?' We had to work our own way through problems, and we learned there was not just one solution," Jessica explains. "He didn't provide answers for us, and we learned more when we had to figure out things for ourselves."

Having the business partner, Eric, interact with the students was a positive addition to the class. Jessica recalls that the students had in-depth discussions with Eric about the project but also about architecture in general. While he didn't solve their problems for them, Eric helped the teams with their assumptions. He was well-versed in the software and his experience in the industry allowed him to give advice such as, "You might do this because the electricians will say . . ."

The presentations were a significant learning experience, as well. There were three teams in her class, and one team presentation was very impressive, showing what was possible. Jessica's team had struggled with some issues; they made the decision to try to do too much in one area, cutting down on the time they had for other tasks. Ted encouraged them to discuss, as part of their presentation, the problems they encountered and how they addressed them. So Jessica came away with a good feeling about the project.

If she could change anything about the class, she'd allot more time for the PBCL activities. The first weeks were smaller assignments, much like the introductory REVIT class, but the difference was that these assignments all built toward the team project. She would like at least a couple of weeks more to become immersed in the real-world problem.

Josh Jones

Josh Jones has taken general education courses at other colleges but now is working on an A.A.S. degree in electrical engineering technology at NSCC. He is employed at Nashville Electric Service and would like to move up in the company. In the Intro to Engineering Technology class, he has experienced problem-based case learning for the first time.

The instructor, Innocent Usoh, used several cases that were developed during The Case Files project to introduce students to various engineering disciplines. Josh liked "Home With a View" best. Though the focus of that particular case was architectural engineering, Josh gained skills that he felt prepared him well for other engineering courses. As a team leader, he discovered that he had leadership potential. "I had to work with a person that I wouldn't have chosen to work with otherwise," Josh says. "I had to understand his strengths." That individual contributed to the group, and Josh was glad that "it forced me to go outside my comfort zone."

He learned from his team members, too. As they worked on "Home With a View," one of the individuals in his group helped him learn Autocad, which he had never used. While his team used Autocad for their drawings, another team used Google Sketch-up.

"In this type of 'hands-on' class you teach yourself a lot of things and you and your team members figure out things for yourselves," he says. Josh liked the fact that the case had many possible solutions.

The cases used in this class include videos with video clips from business partners. Though he sees that there would be value in having a real business partner come to the class, Josh thinks the videos were effective. "It's easy to miss something," he says. "I liked being able to go back to the videos. I watched them over and over." "The class was fun," Josh says, and he looks forward to other classes that use PBCL.

Randall Hayes

A former NSCC graduate in the architectural/engineering technology program, Randall Hayes returned a few semesters ago to take CAD courses at the request of the company that employed him at that time. After he left that company and later experienced a period of unemployment due to the downturn in the economy, he continued to take courses in CAD and REVIT. In his work for several mechanical/plumbing contractors through the years, primarily in the hospital market, he read and interpreted construction drawings. The CAD and REVIT courses will "enhance my ability to do the coordination of trades and layout that I do," Randall says, and make him more marketable.

More than twenty years have elapsed since he received his A.A.S. degree at NSCC. The CAD courses and REVIT 1 were taught much like he expected, in the traditional mode. He was always willing to put in extra time on his projects. He liked to prepare ahead of time, to do the reading that would allow him to get the most from a class. It was not surprising that he excelled in the classes.

Though he also made an "A" in REVIT 2, he points out that his learning style didn't always mesh with the PBCL approach. Some of the reading material was handed out during the classes, as students worked on their problem, and it frustrated Randall that he didn't have the opportunity to prepare adequately before class. His biggest struggle was the lack of time to work on the problem. He liked the idea of an authentic problem but notes that applying concepts to a real situation requires much more time than the kind of assignments given in previous classes.

He admits he was impatient with students who were less serious about class than he was. Working in teams was important to prepare students for teamwork in their jobs, but Randall noted that there were some difficulties. Each person on the team of four was supposed to take one discipline, with the idea that all of the work would mesh in the end, but that process didn't work well for their particular project. Also, Randall was not comfortable teaming with classmates without the experience and focus that he had. "Maybe I'd like a little more teacher control," he says. Some of his observations, he knows, come from being a "seasoned" person with a unique perspective and work ethic.

Randall worried about the grade his team might receive, as opposed to earning an individual grade, but his instructor "had a good handle on that." Ted Kraus used a combination of individual and team grades for the final grade, and the team project was not judged solely on the presentation. "We had operational issues with hardware and software," Randall explains, "but Ted didn't penalize us. He was interested in how we handled the setbacks. We kept forging ahead, as you have to do when something like that happens on the job."

Randall especially liked the discussions with the business partner. "Eric helped us work out glitches," he explains. "Anytime you can bring in someone who's doing what you're learning to do, that's a good thing. What Eric said paralleled and enhanced what Ted had told us, but it meant more coming from the person who's applying it, day in and day out. He gave a real-life perspective."

Mickey King

Mickey King has finished his work at NSCC to obtain the A.A.S. degree in General Technology. While he works as a draftsman at a technology company, he is planning to finish his general education courses at NSCC and go on to a university, where he will prepare to become a teacher. "I've always had the desire to teach," he says. "I just didn't have a plan until now."

Mickey describes the problem-based case learning experience in Ted Kraus's advanced REVIT class as "challenging" and "way different" from other classes. He enjoyed having a real problem to solve and he learned a lot from working in a team. He appreciated being exposed to the team environment because in the real world of work, "you work in teams and the division of responsibilities is clear." His particular team worked well together. "Even though Ted drew names from a hat for the teams, ours was balanced in experience and abilities," Mickey recalls. Some of the teams had problems getting everyone to agree on how to resolve issues, but "our team was great," he says, even though the team concept was new to some of the members.

Perhaps it's because of Mickey's goal to be a teacher that he paid close attention to Ted Kraus's teaching style – the way he presented information and helped the students resolve issues. "Ted was able to create a real learning atmosphere as opposed to the typical and generic 'sit down, shut up and take notes' type of classroom," says Mickey. He describes the teaching style as one that "not only leads the student through a process but at the same time instills self confidence."

"If you had a problem, Ted didn't lecture," Mickey explains. "He'd ask, 'What do you think the problem is? If you did that, what do you think would happen?'" Because of Mickey's previous work experience, he didn't need as much help with technical aspects as other students did, but he says, "I learned from listening to Ted. He encouraged students to ask questions, but he didn't give the answers. He helped them work through the problem to a conclusion." Mickey adds, "When you go through it like that, you don't forget it."

Those critical thinking skills carry over into his present work. "I use them on the job every day," he says. He gives an example of doing a layout and trying to figure out a short cut. "In the back of mind, I could hear Ted saying, 'What are you looking for?' and 'If you do this, what will happen?'

Mickey says he found a short cut that saved quite a bit of time.

Mike Bennett

Mike Bennett has an A.A.S. in Mechanical Engineering and works for an engineering test lab. Mechanical engineering and architecture have been Mike's areas of interest for a long time, and he has taken additional courses in both disciplines, at NSCC and at other institutions, with the goal of eventually working toward a university degree.

The advanced REVIT class, built around problem-based case learning methodology, introduced concepts that Mike indicated were not new to him, given his background, but vitally important for students who are planning to enter the job market. In his present job, Mike is a manager, and he has experience working in teams. He knows that teamwork is part of today's workplace, so the team building skills are useful.

Mike enjoyed having Eric, the business partner, come to the class. "Working with someone in the industry gave us more confidence that this software is actually in demand," he explains. "When we had questions, Eric answered and elaborated with real examples. This pinpointed the more important uses of the program, not just the perceived important functions of the software."

The real-world situation that students had to address provided a project that "was big and scary, and it added excitement to the class," Mike says. "It was really an aggressive project." He notes that "we had some technical issues that ate up class time." Those issues may not come up in future classes. But one thing Mike would suggest, given the scope of the project, is to start earlier. With the outcomes students were expected to achieve, they needed more time than was scheduled for the project. Even after they began working in teams, Mike recalls that "it took too long to get to the drawings."

He also notes, "Sometimes our team members relied on each other too much." Though he understands the value of teamwork in the real world to develop answers, he believes his team's interactions consumed too much time, thus limiting the actual practice and production.

Though he was more experienced than some of the other students, he believes that if they were turned loose on the problem earlier in the semester, "we could have learned the things we needed to know as we worked through the project. We could have dealt with issues as they came up."

Mike says that he achieved his goal for taking REVIT, which was to expand his knowledge base in an area that he liked. "Some students really topped out," he says. For some of them, the class was an introduction to skills and concepts that Mike had previously learned, but he enjoyed the PBCL approach. "The intent was to simulate real-world ideas, and it did that," he says. Comparing the REVIT course to others he has taken through the years, he says, "It was by far a much more accomplished class."

Kristy Johnson

Kristy Johnson was skeptical about the web design class at NSCC. It was a capstone course, in which students would utilize all the skills they had gained in other courses. However, the first class meeting, she realized she was the only student in the class who had a background in building websites. She spoke to her instructor, Dale Rogers, explaining to him that she was already working on websites for a couple of clients. She had registered for the class to expand her skills, but she was concerned about what the class could really offer her, concerned that it might be a waste of her time.

Dale assured her that all the students in the class had strengths to offer, even if they had not built websites previously, and that the class would not be a waste of her time.

PBCL methodology was clear from the beginning, as Dale presented several potential clients from which the class would choose as business partners. Kristy had taken other classes in the visual communication program, working toward her A.A.S. degree, and she recognized that actually working with a business partner would be a new experience. Based on what they understood to be the potential clients' business concepts and website needs, the class settled on two businesses. Dale arranged face-to-face meetings with them.

The class was small, lending itself to only two teams. Both teams put together proposals for their business partners. Kristy's team worked with the owner of Petite Boutique, who had a store in a strip mall. "We communicated with her on a daily basis, using Google groups and emails," Kristy says. "There was a huge amount of work to do. She wanted everything she had in the store to be available on her website." Kristy's team coordinated the content, the descriptions and images, prepared the layout and formatting, and created an online catalog.

"When we made our presentation, she was thrilled," Kristy says.

The PBCL experience helped Kristy develop skills in teamwork, communication, and problem solving. "I learned to take constructive criticism, and I learned that there is not just one right answer." As is often the case in the "real world," the project didn't end for Kristy on the date of the presentation. The client needed help to learn how to maintain her website. Kristy worked with her at her home on some of the operations that she didn't understand.

"When you work with a real business partner, a face-to-face client, you have to take your ego out of the design work. The client has a certain image to project," Kristy explains. "You get the kind of hands-on experience that you couldn't get in a traditional classroom or from a 'make-believe' problem."

The PBCL experience provided an excellent addition to Kristy's portfolio, and she feels exceptionally prepared to work with her present clients and prospective new ones. As for her initial concern that the class might be a waste of time – not so!

Commentaries from Early in PBCL Practice

Several instructors have integrated PBCL processes into their curriculum. Since this program has been active for over twelve years, some of the instructors have had experience with earlier versions of the process.

This section relates experiences that instructors have had with PBCL in various stages of development. Some of the processes and descriptions used during early development have changed slightly as the PBCL experience has been perfected, but please notice that all of them use an active business partner to help define the problem that students use as the basis of their work.

Ed Mummert

Ed Mummert used PBCL in his four-hour Applied Networking class, a capstone course at NSCC. The business partner was a medium-sized church with various networking needs. Their outdated equipment was inadequate; they needed a method for sharing computer data that pertained to the congregation without interfering with sensitive information from the database; and they wanted to network all their computers. Students took initiative, worked outside of class, and exchanged many e-mails with instructor as they came up with questions in the course of their research. They came up with several solutions.

What did we learn from Ed's experience with PBCL?

- Students are more enthusiastic when they encounter a real-world problem and are able to talk with business partner.
- Teams are motivated by the possibility that their solution might actually be implemented.
- The PBCL experience is most successful all around when the business situation meshes well with the objectives of the course. Ed's case was not an "add-on" to the course. It was used to teach what the course was supposed to teach: "New installs, testing cables, all the techniques that we teach in our courses – it was really good for what we do."

Jim Graf

In a four-hour JAVA Applications class at NSCC, Jim Graf introduced his students to a company that owned five sub shops. The company had started out with one store and a "do-by-hand" payroll system that was never upgraded. The business partner came to class and explained the company's needs, showing examples of reports. The class worked to develop an integrated computer system. The business problem became a means by which they learned the JAVA syntax.

What did we learn from Jim's experience with PBCL?

- Students develop the necessary skills to work the problem as they work the problem. Jim initially believed they needed certain basic skills before he introduced the business partner so he waited until half way through the course. He said, "In reality, I could have presented it the first day."
- The instructor should spend adequate time researching the problem ahead of time to scaffold students' learning in the right direction. Scaffolding refers to the growth of students in a particular area. As a student begins to understand the problem at one level, additional complexities can be gradually added. Even though the problem is open-ended, the instructor needs to stay ahead of the students and help them gradually increase their understanding to greater levels of complexity.
- This is one of the very important things that a teacher must do to help students progress in PBCL. It takes a lot of time, effort, and individual attention.

Sam Ruple

In an entry-level programming course at Roane State Community College, students worked with a business partner from a Department of Energy facility. The business partner presented the requirement to develop software to control the movement of machines used to measure the accuracy of the production of nuclear weapons components. The situation itself was highly technical and complex, but Sam extracted from it what could be used with his class.

From the beginning, students were motivated, even those that Sam considered the weakest students. The Learning Cycle helped focus the learning on process skills as well as needed content knowledge. The class was able to experience what it feels like to be a professional programmer working in a real-world setting.

What did we learn from Sam's experience with PBCL?

- It is possible to take a high-level situation and frame the problem for an entry-level class.
- Some content was not covered, but other competencies were added. It is important to be conscious of standards, Sam noted, but the skills acquired through the PBCL experience were, in his words, "maybe more valuable."

Pat Wurth

In a Project Management class at Roane State Community College, Pat Wurth's students learned about the design and development of a GIS (Geographic Information Systems) database, data validation, and spatial analysis. The business problem Pat used for PBCL came from a city government. The city was participating in the Tennessee Base Mapping Program, which was started as a statewide initiative to provide all counties with a standard base map that would seamlessly integrate with all other counties using the same program.

Students worked as a team to develop a procedure for creating shape files for the zones that would be fitted to the new land base backgrounds purchased from the State Base mapping system. They presented a finished solution of 16 separate shape files that were edge-matched to insure they aligned properly with adjacent zone shape files. The business partner commented on their professional delivery and actually implemented their solution.

What did we learn from Pat's experience with PBCL?

- For some business partners, a direct benefit may be realized. In this case, the local newspaper reported in an article about this effort that the students' contribution probably saved the city $25,000.

- The practical, real-world experience students gain through PBCL is valuable when they conduct a job search. Pat's students included in their presentation a color map of the zones they had created and they noted that such a product would be a significant addition to their own portfolios.

Bill Finney

When Bill Finney was getting his Masters Degree in the 1990s, he was introduced to case studies. Shortly after, he began to try to use case studies in the Codes class he was teaching at NSCC. He developed a "made-up" case for the class and saw that it gave students active involvement. Problem-based case learning was a logical next step for Bill. The work he had done for his Codes class put him in a position to take up PBCL and run with it. The leap from "made-up" cases to using a real problem with a real client was one Bill was ready to take. He worked on The Case Files grant, developed cases, and used them effectively in his classes.

His most comprehensive case was "Laughing Child Daycare Center," used in his Architectural Design Process class. The business problem came from a graduate of a business program who wanted to be an entrepreneur and had decided to start a daycare center. She did not have a site, a budget, or any specific details about her requirements. Bill used this business situation in his class to give students real-world experience in determining programmatic information, assessing the information, and using it as the basis to prepare a conceptual design of the facility.

"I'm convinced that students would never have had the opportunity at NSCC to do programming," Bill says. "Even at a university, I don't believe they would have had that depth of experience."

Students worked in teams, developed the skills that they were supposed to gain in the course, and went beyond, learning to "figure out" things for themselves that were not specifically part of the course. PBCL methodology pushed them to find subject matter experts rather than depending on the instructor. For example, students brought in an expert on "green architecture," who presented information on how to design energy-efficient HVAC systems. They learned to take initiative and many experienced being in a leadership role for the first time.

Many at NSCC called Bill Finney the "poster child for PBCL." He embedded PBCL in everything he taught. His goal was to prepare students for the many knowledge gaps they will encounter in the workplace, and he was convinced that the best way to prepare them was through letting them find out things for themselves - without study packets, without safety nets.

Bill took a job with the State of Tennessee, writing contracts for architects who design State projects. He is still a great believer in the value of PBCL, and he knows that if he were still teaching, he'd be making a great effort to bring that type of real-world experience into the classroom. "I'm trying to work with a university professor, hoping he will introduce his students to some real ADA projects," Bill says, "so they will have to learn ADA laws and regulations. If that happens, I'll be putting some of the PBCL methodology into effect."

What did we learn from Bill's experience with PBCL?

- Students were better prepared for the real world of work because their classroom experience closely simulated an architectural office.
- Even the students who seemed ill prepared got more out of the class than expected.
- PBCL gave the students knowledge, skills, and attitudes that transfer to other courses and situations.

Each instructor's experience was unique, but some common themes appeared in all the situations where PBCL was used:

- The expectations of both the instructor and business partner were "in sync." The knowledge, skills, and attitudes found in the business context meshed with the course objectives.
- Students were more engaged when working with a real business partner and a real case that might actually be implemented.
- Students, even in an entry class, were able to develop the necessary skills as they worked the problem.
- Faculty framed the problem to use as a vehicle for learning; it was not an add-on.
- Students transferred the knowledge, skills, and attitudes developed through PBCL to other courses, to job searches, and to the real world of work.

4

BRINGING INDUSTRY INTO THE CLASSROOM

by Dale Rogers
Nashville State Community College

Guest author Dale R. Rogers is an Assistant Professor and Program Coordinator for the Multimedia Concentration at NSCC. He serves as Co-PI of the NSF-funded Innovations in Teaching and Learning (PBCL dissemination grant). In that capacity, he has guided the project in technical matters, strategic planning, and oversight of general operations. As a teacher who uses PBCL in the classroom, he has functioned as an advocate and public speaker for PBCL on the local and community level and at professional conferences throughout the U.S.

Dale came to NSCC with a background is in corporate training. Before coming to NSCC, he worked as a corporate trainer, web designer, and system administrator. He has a B.S. in Mechanical Drafting and Design Technology and a Master's degree in eLearning Design and Technology.

A Case Study In PBCL Course/Business Partner Matching

Problem-Based Case Learning (PBCL) is a teaching method where businesses bring real-world problems into the classroom for solution by students. The instructor acts as a facilitator. I was asked to write a chapter for this book that illustrates my success using PBCL methods in the classroom. Specifically, I have had a lot of success with the Course/Business Partner Matching step in the PBCL Cycle as it applies to my Web and Multimedia Design capstone class. The chapter objective is to illustrate my process so it may help others achieve success.

Motivation

I started the process of inviting businesses into my classroom through my desire to find placements for my students following graduation. As a Program Coordinator and advisor, I consult with students frequently that are in need. Some are straight out of high-school, most are returning adults caught up in layoffs or simple trying to better themselves. Almost all have limited resources and limited time to achieve their goals. Getting them prepared for a career in Web Design or Multimedia Design is my challenge so they can earn a decent living for themselves and their families.

I attended several presentations at NSCC where Program Coordinators and Deans were talking about how they had developed relationships with large employers to provide a path to employment. Many of these positions were maintenance or line workers at manufacturing plants. As plants automate they need an army of skilled technicians to keep everything running smoothly. I did not find this approach to be effective for my discipline and student population. Most small to medium size organizations will only employ one web designer. Once the initial design is complete, the designer's primarily role is in maintaining the web site. While web sites are an important part of everyday life and business, finding placements for my graduates would need a different approach than grooming them for sparse corporate positions.

At the same time I was scanning the horizon for potential employers, my phone was frequently ringing with calls from local small businesses and start-ups seeking students to create web sites as a school project. Up to that point, the position of the department was to refer the phone calls to the Career Services Department so the students' engagement could be monitored by the school. Without faculty scaffolding, however, it was hard to determine what learning, if any, was taking place. I slowly began realizing that it was small business that held the most promise for creating the jobs and opportunities for my graduates. I needed to engage local small businesses intelligently, both for their safety and for the safety of my students. I wanted to model good business skills for my students.

After much thought, I came upon the idea of creating a classroom experience that mimicked an apprenticeship or internship. The business partners had a real time actual business problem to be solved; i.e. they needed a web site or presentation and lacked the design background. My students have the design background and need the experience of working in the field and solving design problems from the beginning to end. They need to build their portfolio. Lastly, they need a facilitator or guide to hold their hand, if needed, through the process. My answer was my capstone class.

Knowing the Outcomes

Before I could approach small businesses, I had to be very clear about what I wanted out of the relationship. I had the advantage of creating a new curriculum. I was in charge of designing the courses and outcomes to prepare the students for their careers. Therefore I had a lot of leeway in which classes were needed and what the courses, and program, outcomes should be.

The capstone class is the last class in the curriculum. It is the culmination of all the classes that have been taken. The idea for a capstone is simple: the student will use all the skills they have acquired through their program to create a project with minimal help. It enables the student to transfer their knowledge to application. It enables them to feel confident in problem solving. It allows the faculty to monitor student achievement and see where the strengths and weaknesses are in the program.

My challenge was to create the course so business partners would supply the problem and engage with the students throughout the process. I would act both as a project manager, and ultimately as a teacher who assigns a grade based on a rubric.

The Capstone's Needs Analysis

Faculty never work in a vacuum. There are many stakeholders that need to be considered when designing a course. The course needs to fit in the larger vision of the program outcomes. If the course does not meet a need in the program outcomes, it is superfluous and needs to be eliminated. It also has to meet the requirements of the educational governing body, in the case of my institution, that is TBR (Tennessee Board of Regents).

The course has to work within the immediate or nuclear institution as well, i.e. Nashville State Community College. Nashville State's prime initiative, at the time of this course's creation, was to design courses that can document student progress in the area of critical thinking. Since authentic problem-solving is rich in critical thinking, that should not have been a problem. The challenge would be in capturing that progress and finding a way to document it. What were the indicators?

The course needed to address the following items:

- Give 2-year community college students an internship experience.
- Experience must be in the classroom to allow working adults to participate in real-world projects.
- Give students the opportunity to expand their soft-skills; i.e. working in groups, communication skills, time management, organization, etc.
- Assess students as a group and also as individuals.
- Provide a venue to monitor how successfully the student has met the program outcomes.

Figure 4:
The Course Structure:

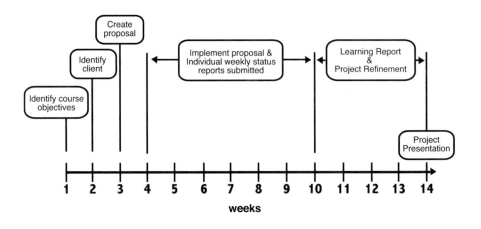

PROBLEM-BASED CASE LEARNING

Understand that no course is frozen in time. I first brought business partners into the classroom in Spring of 2008 and as of this writing (Spring 2011) my students have created 9 web sites for a variety of customers, 2 online videos for one small business (currently on their web site), 1 podcast for a national competition, and 1 DVD for the Nashville Area Habitat for Humanity. As I get more acquainted with the needs of my community, the capabilities of my students, and become more experienced at designing better assessment tools, the course continues to evolve. With that said, Figure 4 outlines the course structure at this moment in time.

The capstone course is a semester-long course that lasts approximately fourteen weeks. It meets once a week for three hours. The three-hour class is not lecture time. It is the time that is used for face-to-face interaction. That may be meeting the business partner. It may be outlining the problems to be solved using the PBCL spiral and Need to Know Board. It may be reviewing concepts that are needed to solve a problem. It's mostly an open discussion about whatever the students need at that moment to get the project completed on time.

Week One

The first week introduces the students to the PBCL method of teaching. Since the method is more experiential with the instructor playing a facilitation role, the students need to be prepared for the instructor playing a different role than what they are used to. It tends to throw students off at first. They are mostly concerned with knowing exactly what they need to do in order to get a passing grade. This is the time to introduce the grading rubric and the over-all structure of the class. Since most of the semester is about group work, names and contact information are exchanged. I inform the students that a business partner will be present for the next class, so throughout the week, create a questionnaire to use to get whatever information you need to start the design of the client's web site.

During the first week's class session, we create a common online working space for questions to be added and a discussion to take place. As of this writing, the tool we use is Google Docs and Google Groups. Every student has access to both and we confirm the students' ability to access the spaces before they leave the room.

Week Two

By the second week, two clients have been chosen and the students have created questionnaires as a group. I will address finding a client in a separate section of this chapter. The clients come into the class, talk about their needs, get to know everyone, and answer the questions that the students have developed. Depending on the communication skills of everyone in the room this can take anywhere from an hour to the entire class period. I reserve about half an hour at the end to set next week's milestones and activities.

You may notice in the above paragraph that I said two clients are chosen. Sometimes clients are not available. Regardless of how many emails or phone calls we send out, a client is sometimes noncompliant to our requests for content, feedback, or whatever, due to either professional or personal reasons. Rather than be dead in the water, the class works with two clients. In that way they learn to juggle projects. We have never had a case where both clients' were MIA (Missing in Action) at the same time. Usually the absent client resurfaces with apologies and a renewed vigor in the process.

Week Three

The third week is when we create a proposal. It is when we discuss as a group what the client needs and what we, as a group, feel confident that we can provide. We set expectations, legal responsibility, scope of work, and also make sure the client knows that the project may not be completed, or completed to their satisfaction. I provide the proposal template. We select a client liaison and a good editor to take charge of the proposal creation. By next week, the proposal must be completed and ready for signatures including limitation of scope and responsibility and projected timelines and milestones. The liaison emails the document to the client for approval and signature. The signature page is faxed back to the instructor (or liaison) for student and instructor signatures. Everyone gets a copy. With the proposal firmly in place, the next six weeks are about implementing the promises made in the proposal.

It is important to not that to avoid institutional liability, I copied the my Dean and Vice-President of Academic Affairs to ensure I wasn't overstepping any bounds, entering into a contract that might involve the Tennessee Board of Regents or Nashville State Community College. The contract was sent to TBR legal for feedback. Small changes were made by legal to protect the State from liability. I incorporated the changes before sending to the client for signatures.

Weeks Four-Ten

During each weekly class period between weeks four through ten, students are engaged in problem solving. Early in my process, I tried stepping back and allowing the students to guide the process. What I found was that most students do not have the project and time management skills to lead the process. It created a lot of confusion and stress since no one had a clue of where to start. They were dependent on the instructor for structure. So I gave it to them. Now, I lead the project, assigning tasks as I go. This ensures that everyone sees the big picture, has a say in how things are accomplished, knows what they are expected to do individually, and can also monitor the progress of the project as a whole.

The number of groups I create is dependent on the size of the class. My program, Multimedia and Web Design, is still a relatively small program as it is growing completely by word of mouth. My capstone classes started off in Spring 2008 with three web design students. The last one in Spring of 2010 had seven students consisting of three web design and four multimedia students. The three web design students focused on the web design aspect of the project. The four multimedia students focused on the media creation, i.e. two videos that would be included on the web site. The group of four multimedia students shot the footage, wrote the script, produced the videos, and determined the best technology to use to embed them in the web pages. Flash was chosen as the preferred platform. All students had the opportunity to give feedback, offer suggestions, and play a role if desired. Each week students are required to submit a weekly status report in the template I provide. The status report helps me stay abreast of issues happening in the project and the challenges the students are facing.

Week Ten: The Learning Report

By week ten the project is well underway and should be nearing completion. The ability to meet the milestones determines whether everything is finished by week ten or whether there are still loose ends to tie up. Regardless of the state of the project, a new task is introduced.

Up to week ten, all the students work as a group. Starting in week ten, in addition to finishing up their responsibilities on the group project, they are now responsible for creating a Learning Report. The Learning Report is an individual assignment and must address the following:

- Describe the Project.
- Describe your role in the Project.
- Address the challenges you encountered and how you overcame those challenges.
- Link your activities back to your program curriculum, i.e. which courses helped you the most as you were actively engaged in problem solving.
- Why are you ready to graduate?
- What value are you bringing to an employer?

Dr. John Bransford's research into how people learn indicates that students learn more deeply when they monitor their learning; which is a metacognitive process. Reflection on learning is part of the PBCL method. The Learning Report provides reflection and is the metacognitive part of the process and is published in a medium that is relative to the student's major. Web Design students produce a web site learning report. Multimedia students produce a learning report in a podcast, video-podcast, movie, Keynote, PowerPoint or Prezi (www.prezi.com) presentation platform. Whatever the medium, the presentation includes images, sound, video, animations, transitions, and can be executed on a web page. One student used Prezi with outstanding results.

The Last Week: Formal Presentations
The last week is reserved for presentations. A formal presentation is arranged. The business partners, members of the school administration, faculty, students, advisory committee members, and local employers are invited to attend. A brief survey is distributed so that audience members can take notes on outstanding elements they observe and areas where a student can improve. The surveys are anonymous and are turned into the instructor at the completion of the event.

Before the last week, we discuss as a group who will lead the presentation. Each student will have a chance in front of the audience talking about their role and challenges, but one or two students will be in charge of leading the process.

Finding Business Partners

Business partners are everywhere. Locating and retaining them is an ongoing challenge. In the beginning I developed a relationship with the Tennessee Small Business Development Center. Its director at the time, Paula Roberts, was very open to what I was doing and found two members of the center to engage my classroom. (A video interview with Roberts can be found on http://www.makinglearningreal.org. Navigate to PBCL in the Classroom>Four Classrooms>Dale Rogers.) Two semesters later Paula Roberts left the TSBDC for another position in the community. I tried to contact the current director with no results. I began looking for other partners.

In Spring 2010 I secured two business partners for my capstone class through personal contacts. One of my colleagues at the college, Cliff Rockstead, teaches in the Entrepreneurship program. He is a strong advocate for what I am accomplishing. One of his friends is Ernie Gendron, the owner of Alternator Starter Parts Distributors. Ernie, Cliff, and I met at a local Starbucks for coffee during the previous semester. Ernie explained that he was bringing his newly acquired company back from the brink of collapse from the previous owner. He had a great service, was employing local people, and wanted to take the business nationally. To do this he desperately needed a web site. I spoke to him about what I needed to accomplish and he was on board. You can see the results of the work for Ernie at http://www.alternatorstarterpartsdistributors.com. Watch the videos to see what the multimedia students accomplished. The web site was designed by the web design students.

I teach an Adobe Flash course. One of my students in a previous semester's Flash class was the Art Director for one of the leading design agencies in Nashville, Bohan Advertising (http://www.bohanideas.com) I approached this student about whether Bohan would be interested in partnering with me for my capstone class. She put me in touch with her management team and I arranged an interview. The second client for the Spring 2010 Capstone Class was Bohan Advertising. We completed a project for one of their clients, the Salama Institute (http://www.salamaserves.org).

I met with an Account Manager at Bohan and presented what I wanted to do. In PBCL we strive for the middle third. The middle third is a project that is not critical to the success of the client but is still important enough to pursue.

Top Third	Mission critical. Company absolutely needs the project to succeed.
Middle Third	Not critical but desired. The project would help the bottom line but not harm the company if it wasn't completed.
Lower Third	Project is not important enough to pursue.

To have a company fail because of our students' efforts would be unacceptable and too risky. A project in the lower third is not preferable because it is so unimportant that the likelihood of having a business partner devote time and resources to it are slim. The middle third takes the pressure of everyone yet is interesting enough to engage the students and the partner in the process to see the project succeed.

Bohan had a client they were doing pro-Bono work for. Salama Institute, near downtown Nashville, works with children in after school activities and has limited resources for marketing. Since the work was pro-Bono, Bohan did not have the same time restrictions that they would with a paying client. A Bohan Account Manager acted as the company liaison with Salama. The students created the project under the guidance of the Bohan Account Manager. When the project got far enough along that Salama needed to engage, the students were introduced to the representative at Salama to refine and finish the process.

I'm always looking and thinking where my business partner will come from. I talk about my program in many different settings and collect business cards from people that appear interested. Thus far, I have not found an instance where a business partner was not available when I needed one.

The General Process

I use the same basic approach each time I look for business partners to engage in the classroom:

- Identify the needs in the community that relate to the discipline and keep my eye out for potential business partners.
- WIIFM - Identifying what's in it for all stakeholders so you create buy-in for everyone.
- Be very clear about what the needs of the course in terms of outcomes and criteria.
- Be very clear about what services you and your students can realistically provide.
- Be very clear about the needs of the educational institution.
- Be very clear about the needs and capabilities of your students.

Understand that it is a process and mistakes will be made. Keep expectations moderate so the mistakes aren't catastrophic. Don't forget it's a class and learning is more important than project perfection. Remember the middle third.

The Pitch

The PBCL process is a win-win-win process; a win for the business partner, a win for the college, a win for the student. Make sure you represent that in your pitch to the business partner.

The Proposal

Set expectations for everyone. Keep yourself, your students, and the institution free from liability. Keep the promises simple so you can achieve the goal.

The Implementation

Keep everyone on track. Use the proposal and the PBCL learning cycle as your guide. Accomplish what you promised in the proposal. Make sure you pay attention to the grading rubric. You only want to emphasize the important skills.

The Presentation

Students can be too honest and not emphasize their strengths. Review the learning report before the presentation. Help the students learn to represent themselves in a favorable light.

The Follow up

Maintain relationships with the students and with the business partners.

- How are they coming along?
- Was the project a success over time?
- Do the students need help as they go into the work place?

I stay in contact with my students through Facebook and LinkedIn. They still come to me, after graduation, for advice, and I send clients and job opportunities to them as I hear about them. Successful education, like any other endeavor, requires good customer service skills. The students will come back and speak well of the program once they are in the field. The business partners will spread the word in the community.

My Background

I left this section for the last so it did not interfere with the discussion of PBCL. My background is in corporate training. After graduating with a B.S. in Mechanical Drafting and Design Technology from Alabama A&M University, I worked for the Intergraph Corporation in Huntsville Alabama as an instructor. I designed a 5-day class, teaching engineers and architects how to use the Project Engineer Pipe 3D piping design software.

I left Intergraph after 5 years and moved to Nashville where I worked as a corporate trainer teaching Microsoft office (specializing in database design and Microsoft Access), Windows OS, and Web Design classes. I was also the company's Web Designer and assistant System's Admin. After that I worked for Vanderbilt University has a Program Assistant and Web Designer for a Doctoral Program in Reliability and Risk Engineering in the Civil and Environmental Department. Before coming to Nashville State Community College (NSCC) I was eighteen credits into a Master's Degree in eLearning Design and Technology.

The reason I explain my background is because all students and practitioners come to PBCL with a history. My history included years of experience working with professionals to transfer their classroom instruction back into the workplace. As mentioned elsewhere in the book, faculty that have industry experience have a higher success rate with PBCL. I not only had industry experience, but also industry training experience. I believe that put me at an advantage when it comes to bridging the gap between industry and academia.

The First Year in Academia: Learning How to Assess

In the corporate world, assessments are just as hit and miss as they are in academia. Students, or employees, take a class. They are introduced to concepts, software, procedures, protocols, policies, etc with the hope that they will be able to transfer that knowledge back into their work activities.   From my experience, sometimes the training transferred, sometimes it didn't. Both academia and corporate training rely on quizzes and surveys to help a student (and others) determine if they "got it." Capturing understanding through a quiz is rudimentary at best, and understanding is itself different than applying what you understand. Outside academia, grades are rarely given. A Certificate of Completion is what you get for attending a five-day intensive course. The proof of understanding is how you are able to apply the information once you get back to the office.

Within the first year in my role as full-time faculty in Visual Communications at NSCC, I began hearing faculty and Deans talk about how local industry was dissatisfied with the critical thinking capacities of our graduates. I pressed for the source of that feedback and for details on what critical thinking meant to different stakeholders. I received a smattering of answers. Mostly, it appeared that the feedback came from Advisory Committee members and from employer surveys. No one was able to provide a clear definition of what critical thinking meant to those employers.

An opportunity arose for me to become involved in Nashville State's Critical Thinking Initiative by joining the QEP (Quality Enhancement Plan) Committee, and I took it. The QEP was a required element of accreditation and addressed some area the institution felt could be improved. The challenge of increasing critical thinking skills in our students was chosen as the goal. This was the skill that most lacking in our graduates. I reasoned this was a good place to look for my answers.

One of the first things I noticed once I joined the committee was there was no industry representative at the table. The committee was composed of faculty and administrators. When I asked about this, I was told that industry feedback had been collected prior to my joining the committee. "Critical thinking," I was informed, was the term that industry used to describe the student inadequacy we were trying to address.

In the process of determining how to "fix" this problem, a common definition for "critical thinking" had to be adopted. The committee adopted a definition for critical thinking that had its roots in philosophy and logic. According to Moore, Brook, and Parker (2001), critical thinking is the "careful and deliberate determination of whether to accept, reject, or suspend judgment." The committee decided that the California Critical Thinking test would be the objective standard that the institution would use to determine if our students were being provided the requisite training in critical thinking; irrespective of the discipline. As a faculty member in Visual Communications, I pondered how I would how I was going to work that definition into a Web Design curriculum.

While my efforts with the committee were underway, I also began speaking with my advisory committee and industry acquaintances. I wanted to get a more clear idea of what they meant when they used the phrase "critical thinking." While the term critical thinking was employed in a number of conversations, when I tried to pin down what they meant by critical thinking, it appeared to me that problem solving was really the issue in question. For example, one employer relayed the following story:

The employer had hired a recent male graduate for a programming position. He found that the young man was quite capable in his discipline. He understood the tasks given to him and could finish the programming tasks with no problems. The issue came after he finished the tasks. Rather than contact his supervisor to get another programming task, he started playing video games.

The employer was dismayed that anyone would be so un-thoughtful and believed that this was a sign of faulty critical thinking. I asked the employer if the new hire had gone through an orientation process. He had not. It was clear that the young man knew programming. He could read, listen, and understand what was required of him. He could complete a task, with minimal supervision.

From where I was standing, college had served him well. Beyond the capacity to complete the task, it was up to the employer to set the expectations in the work place. To me, it was not an issue of critical thinking; it was a matter of understanding what the workplace protocols were. That was the employer's responsibility, not academia.

That being said, I myself had plenty of instances in my own classrooms where students were not able to complete an activity, unaided, even though they had completed the requisite course that should have prepared them. That was a transfer issue. I also heard stories from our advisory committee that graduates were unable to complete design tasks without a lot of supervision. They could not work independently. That, I believe, could be mitigated by introducing unstructured application in the coursework and is a perfect example of the strength of the PBCL method of instruction.

My Introduction to PBCL

Dr. Jim Johnson, the Principal Investigator (PI) of the PBCL dissemination grant, at the time of my hire, was the Supervising Dean of my Dean, Karen Stevenson. I knew of his grant only remotely and was too busy getting my bearings in a new position with the college. When I started bring business partners into the classroom, Karen told me that what I was doing was very similar to what Dr. Johnson was doing and that I should talk to him and show him what I was doing. I did.

What I found was an entire structure and community of practice that was trying to accomplish exactly what I was trying to do. There was a decade's worth of research to back it up, mentors to help me refine my process, and a community waiting to engage with me to learn from my successes. I began incorporating more of the PBCL process and tools into my classroom with great success. As I got more involved in the process I was asked to join the grant staff, which led to my current role as Co-PI.

Conclusions

PBCL is not for every instructor. Instructors that don't have industry experience sometimes lack the "comfortability" to approach and engage the business world. Implementing PBCL in the classroom requires that an instructor step into the background and let the process lead. PBCL requires flexibility in designing a rubric and identifying the observable behaviors that can be assigned a grade. Developing assessment instruments are time consuming and require adjustment. In general, it takes more time and energy developing and implementing a course using PBCL.

PBCL is also not for every situation. Some fundamental classes can benefit from the tools PBCL uses to teach and guide authentic problem solving, i.e. the PBCL cycle and Need-to-Know Board. However, the key ingredient in PBCL is engagement of a business partner in the classroom to solve problems. When the students do not have the prerequisite domain knowledge to solve real business problems, attracting a business partner into the classroom is much more difficult since the partner's WIIFM is missing.

If the discipline is appropriate for business engagement, you have a willing business partner with a problem squarely in the middle third, you have students with the requisite skills, and a willing instructor who can lead when necessary and lay back when appropriate, the amount of partner and student engagement can be astounding. The demonstration of student achievement is very clear and public. The institution and the program become well known in the community for capable graduates.

5

THE BUSINESS COMPONENT OF PBCL

by Ted Kraus
Nashville State Community College

Guest author Ted Kraus is an adjunct instructor in the CAD department at Nashville State Community College (NSCC) and the coordinator of the NSF funded Innovations in Teaching and Learning (ITL) grant that is housed at NSCC. He recently received his Masters of Education from Belmont University's Organizational Leadership and Communication Program.

Before returning to school to pursue his Masters, Ted worked in the field of technical theatre, ending his career as the Technical Director of the TONY Award winning Alliance Theatre Company in Atlanta, GA. Ted's thesis, "Methods and Rationale for Using Technical Theatre to Teach Metacognitive and Critical Thinking Skills," reflects his past love of the theatre and his ongoing interest in exploring ways to create contextual learning environments that promote the development of metacognitive and critical thinking skills in students.

One of the most frequently asked questions during a PBCL training workshop is "Where do I find the business partner?" In fact, this question is so pervasive and can seem so daunting that some participants find it difficult to move beyond this fundamental question, even as they recognize the potential benefits of implementing the PBCL strategy. And the question is certainly valid. Because many of the educators who participate in our workshops have never thought to look at the business community as an active partner in their classrooms, determining how to find and then approach a business partner to take part in this joint venture is an important skill to acquire.

But as important as this question is to the implementation of the PBCL strategy, it can perhaps obfuscate an even more basic question that seems harder to voice: "How do I use the business partner in my class?" Once voiced, the question seems obvious, but it can be a very challenging one to answer. Inherent in this question are other questions about what form the new learning environment will take. Ultimately, however, the more effectively one can answer this as-of-yet-unspoken question, the easier it becomes to answer the original question: "Where do I find the business partner?"

As we have seen in other chapters in this book, there are certain classes that lend themselves more easily to implementing the PBCL strategy. Certainly, a capstone course taken at the end of a program of study, designed to give students an opportunity to codify the knowledge they have gathered throughout their time in that program of study, is a good example of a setting that is ripe for using the PBCL methodology.

But what about a class that occurs earlier in a program, where there is still information to be taught to the students, and where successful transmission of that information will have a bearing on classes that the student will take later in the program? Experiences of several instructors who are featured in this book indicate that PBCL can be effectively used throughout the educational process, in introductory and intermediate classes, as well as in capstone classes. However, to do so effectively, the educator must first clearly identify and understand what he or she hopes to achieve by engaging in the partnership being formed.

The need to identify what you, the educator, need to get from the business partner is a step that can be overshadowed by the more practical questions that are involved with actually finding and approaching a business partner. This is especially true in disciplines where the range of choices of business partners seems to be limited, or at the very least, less obvious.

Take, as a comparison, two educators who have been mentioned in this book. The first, Dale Rogers, uses PBCL in his capstone Web-Design classes with great success. The second, Jack Wallace, uses

PBCL effectively in his Architectural Design Process class. These two classes represent two completely different types of environments, and the products produced represent two very different levels of need to the business partner/client.

One could argue that there are more business owners who are willing to let students design their websites than there are business owners (or individuals) that would be willing to let a group of students design their new building. Not only are there licensing issues involved with the architectural process, but also, the finished design for a building represents an end product that is "mission critical," and is therefore beyond the scope of what should be taken on in a class implementing PBCL. The websites that Dale's classes are designing are certainly important to the business partner/client, but they are not "mission critical." Dale would not, for instance, partner with someone who is trying to develop the next "Facebook" or "MySpace," because in these cases, the website would be the major focus of the business.

So the question remains: How do these two instructors, teaching in two disparate disciplines, both manage to function effectively within the PBCL framework? The answer lies in their ability to clearly define what it is that they need to achieve over the course of the semester, and then finding a way to introduce a business partner who can further those goals into the classroom environment.

In order to answer these two fundamental questions defined at the beginning of the chapter, I sent out a survey to a small number of PBCL practitioners who use the PBCL strategy while teaching non-capstone classes. These practitioners were sent a five-question questionnaire that focused on their process during the planning stages of their course work and specifically on how they envisioned using the business partner in the classroom. The practitioners surveyed included teachers from English, math, architecture, and computer sciences.

The survey questions are listed here, and the answers will be summarized throughout the pages that follow:

1. When you approached your business partner, did you have a clear idea regarding what you wanted/needed from your business partner?

2. Did you know what topics you wanted/needed to cover over the course of the semester?
3. Did you tell your business partner what the goals for the semester were?
4. How did you envision your business partner interacting with your class? In other words, did you have a plan when you approached the potential business partner?
5. How did that plan change after you found and engaged your business partner?

Summary of the Survey Results

In response to question 1, 85% of the respondents said that they did have a very clear idea of what they needed from their business partner. Those in the 15% group who said that they did not have a clear idea acknowledged that they had some kind of general concept of what the students were going to do, but they felt the need to leave the role of the business partner more open-ended. Of the 85% that said they did have a clear vision, 33.3% acknowledged using the initial conversations with the business partner to more clearly define what the business partner was offering to the class.

In response to questions 2 and 3, all of the respondents acknowledged that they had a clear understanding or picture of what topics they needed to cover over the course of the semester. This is an important point. Unlike the structure of a typical capstone class, which is designed to give students an opportunity to codify previously-taught material, these classes were tasked with having to teach students new material. For most of the survey participants, this resulted in engaging in some sort of lecture-based interaction with the class. Integrating lectures into a PBCL format can seem antithetical to a new PBCL practitioner, but in some cases it is necessary to do so.

The responses for question 4 were the most varied, with only 66% of the respondents choosing to have the business partners engage with the class directly on a regular basis. However, a full 85% of the respondents had the business partners come into the class at the outset to present a general overview of the topic or project, thus helping to frame the subject matter that would be covered throughout the semester. This way of framing the problem adds a high level of energy to the classroom environment and is one of the key elements of the PBCL strategy.

The response to question 5 was unanimous. All of the respondents said that their plans for how to use the business partner changed after the initial contact was made. In the words of one of them, "There is a constant flux of information and changing parameters as the students ask questions and explore the problem cases."

Analysis of the Survey Results

What the responses of questions 2 through 4 indicate is that these practitioners used their business partners to help create the context within which the topic would be studied. In other words, they used the business partner and the unsolved problem that the business partner provided to "frame" the context of the classroom. This is a critical point, because this way of framing the question is at the core of the PBCL process. In fact, if we look at the cycle as depicted on the Making Learning Real website (www.makinglearningreal.org), we see that what the practitioners surveyed have done brings us through the first four stages of the cycle. These four stages are:

1. **Course/Business Matching**
   The instructor and business partner identify a problematic situation that supports curriculum goals. They then identify the place(s) in the course where the problematic situation should form the context for learning.

2. **Framing**
   The instructor, possibly with help from the business partner, structures the problem so it is adaptable to the student work environment; the problem becomes a vehicle for learning.

3. **The Situation**
   The instructor, often together with the business partner, introduces the students to the business, the problematic situation and the PBCL Cycle. The students begin their quest to uncover the messy problem within the situation.

4. Problem Analysis

Teams of students explore facts, assumptions, questions and resources as they form hypotheses about the underlying problem.

When considering the results of question 5, we see another fundamental aspect of working with the PBCL strategy; that is the need for flexibility. Once the business partner and the subsequent business problem are introduced into the classroom, a great many more variables come into play. In fact, at times it feels like the process of framing the problem has done little more than create a forum for a more chaotic exchange of ideas. It is important that the new PBCL practitioner understand that this way of teaching is messier than a traditional lecture-based class, but that much of the energy and power of the strategy comes from this messiness. As the students take more ownership of the process of answering the business partner's question, and subsequently control of their learning, they begin to create the structure within which the learning is taking place. The "messiness" diminishes as the students start to implement their structures and their solutions.

As this new structure is developing, the role of the teacher is changing. The teacher is now stewarding the students through their learning, as opposed to directing it. As the students move through this process, they are discovering the questions they need to answer, as well as developing a process of problem solving that is more personalized than the traditional classroom experience. In such an environment, however, it is essential that the teacher stay flexible and open to initially giving up some control, as the new structures take shape.

This is not to suggest that there is no room for lectures in a classroom setting based on the PBCL strategy. In fact, there needs to be room for lectures if we hope to implement the PBCL strategy in non-capstone classes.

I am an educator who implements the PBCL strategy in a class that requires me to present my students with new information. And I like to lecture, so I would not want to move to an approach that eliminates the need for lectures altogether. I have found, though, that when I use the PBCL format to frame the context of the subject matter, my students' thinking seems more fluid and they appear to be better able to make conceptual leaps than students who take part in classes that employ only lectures and lab time. The power of PBCL comes from creating a powerful context within which the subject matter is being framed.

At the beginning of this chapter, I identified two questions that are of the utmost importance when looking to implement the PBCL teaching strategy. The first was "Where do I find the business partner?" and the second was "How do I use the business partner in the classroom?" I posited that the second question is really a more fundamental question to answer, because any business partner whom you approach will need to understand his or her role in the process.

What follows is a list of steps one can go through to determine how to use the business partner in the classroom.

- Clarify the curriculum goals for the semester.
- Once identified, work with the business partner to find an unsolved business problem that will satisfy the needs of your semester's curriculum.
- Use your business partner and the business problem to create a context within which to explore the curriculum.
- Have the class analyze the question with the goal of identifying and codifying the semester goals.
- Have the business partner be available to students as a resource throughout the course to answer questions and clarify any issues.
- Have the business partner come back at the end of the case for the student teams' presentations, to offer feedback on the results.

Even with this fundamental question answered, it can still be difficult to know how to find and then approach a business partner. It is a very hard question to answer, given the scope of the disciplines that are implementing the PBCL strategy and differences that exist from school to school and from department to department.

Some departments have active advisory boards while others do not. Some disciplines produce end products that are easier to quantify, and that can make it easier to identify a business partner. That having been said, though, here is a list that outlines some broad stroke recommendations for identifying a business partner for use in your classroom.

- Identify what you need from the business partner you are approaching, as previously outlined.
- Use your advisory committees, alumni organizations, local Chamber of Commerce, local Small Business Administration, technical consultants, and even your adjunct faculty to find likely candidates to approach.
- Use the information you gathered while completing step one on this list to come up with a statement and/or a questionnaire that will help you articulate to the potential business partner what your needs are, what you hope to get from them, and what they can hope to get from you. This point is very important, because this is a partnership. As much as possible, both parties need to be getting something out of this relationship.
- Once a business partner has decided to join you, the same questionnaire can then be used to formulate the business problem that best suits your needs. Again, the clearer you can be about what type of questions you need to have the business problem prompt, the easier it will be for your business partner to help you.
- You are now in the PBCL cycle, as defined on the website: www.makinglearningreal.org.

Finding the business partner can seem daunting and overwhelming when you first begin to consider using the PBCL process, so much so that you may preemptively decide that it is too much trouble to even attempt. That would certainly be a fair conclusion to make. Implementing the PBCL strategy does require some effort, and a different way of first imagining and then managing your classroom. It also produces some very powerful results for your students in the realm of critical thinking and metacognition. The PBCL process forces the students out their comfort zone and into a world where not only the answer is important, but the process of how they arrived at the answer is of utmost importance.

The student, either individually or in a group setting, is getting the opportunity to thoroughly experience and investigate his or her decision making process. The addition of the business partner energizes the classroom and gives the students an opportunity to experience learning on a different level.

6

TEACHER TRAINING FOR PBCL

Most teachers claim that PBCL has been an effective learning technique for their students. However, not all teachers find that presenting PBCL to a class comes naturally for them. Teachers are typically more accustomed to lecturing about a business problem than they are in helping students develop a solution to one. Throughout the twelve years of our project series, our project staff have learned as much about implementing PBCL as the teachers have.

Reemphasizing what can be seen in the PBCL Cycle, the process begins with a partnership, usually stimulated by the teacher, in which a business partner helps to define a current, authentic, business problem that the students will work on. In all of the teacher workshops our project team has conducted, the outline begins in the same way. Local business partners are brought in to work with the teachers to define a realistic business problem that they will develop as a PBCL exercise during the workshop.

Of course, all teachers come to their teaching positions via different paths. Some begin their teaching careers directly after graduating from college. They may have very limited direct experience with business operations. Others have come to teaching due to a career path change. They may have been successful in some aspect of business such as accounting, architecture, construction management, computer operations, electrical/electronics, manufacturing, or a long list of other business and technical careers.

Teachers with business backgrounds adapt to using the PBCL method of teaching very quickly because the process is almost second nature to them. The teachers who have had little business experience in their careers can quickly learn how to relate to business operations through discussions with their business partners.

Some of the most valuable Case Files that were developed were in the area of mathematics. On the web site, www.thecasefiles.org, a valuable case was developed by a couple of math teachers at NSCC in partnership with a local business. In this case, students used real-life examples to develop a graphical analysis in which the slope of the graph had special significance.

After working with this case, students were found to have learned the concept of graphical analysis very well, but, even more importantly, they were able to apply the concepts to other similar situations. The person leading the development of this case file was a very competent math teacher but had little experience working with or for businesses.

Even though the methods of PBCL may be more familiar to teachers in technology fields, teachers in academic areas should not avoid using PBCL because the need to apply the academic skills is extremely important for students' success in the workplace. PBCL allows students to learn to use academic skills while solving technical problems. The integration of these skills is extremely important to the success of all students regardless of their chosen field of specialization.

Through many teacher training events, we learned that the PBCL process is best learned through an immersion process where the teachers work in small groups and can easily discuss, reflect and provide feedback on the situation being presented by the business partner. A good example is an ABC video presented on Nightline on July 13, 1999, called "DEEP DIVE: The Shopping Cart."

The primary message of the video is innovation leading to product design. The example studies a group of designers who have various skills and background such that each of them sees a problem from a unique viewpoint. Their goal, as a team, is to design a new style shopping cart that would outperform all others currently in use. After a large group meeting to define the project goals, the designers work in small groups to gather as much background information about the project as possible. This takes a significant amount of research and observations. When all of the designers reconvene, they share ideas, thoughts and insights that they have acquired. After a relatively short amount of time, each small group of the design team presents several examples of shopping carts for the rest of the team to consider. Following a frank discussion, the design team selects one design, the one they feel best meets the requirements, to present to the customer.

Even though this example was developed over a decade ago, the video is still available from ABC and has been one of the bestselling videos of the entire Nightline series. It also illustrates what has been called "an immersion process" where participants become engaged in solving a problem and not listening to a lecture about it.

Personal engagement is the quality illustrated in the last example. It is extremely important, from a motivational standpoint, to get students (albeit in this example the students are teachers themselves) engaged with the solution. To use their own personal experience to help understand the problem and to develop a possible solution is extremely important.

All students bring with them a wealth of individual experiences and knowledge that can be applied toward a solution to the problem. In teams, they make proposals for possible solutions and present their plans to fellow students who offer feedback. What emerges in the process is a depth of knowledge about content, practice with learning process, and an opportunity to reflect on their own and others' presented solutions, which is metacognition. Rather than memorizing facts and concepts, they use content knowledge and skills to clarify, create, critique ideas and processes.

Figure 5:
Training Levels

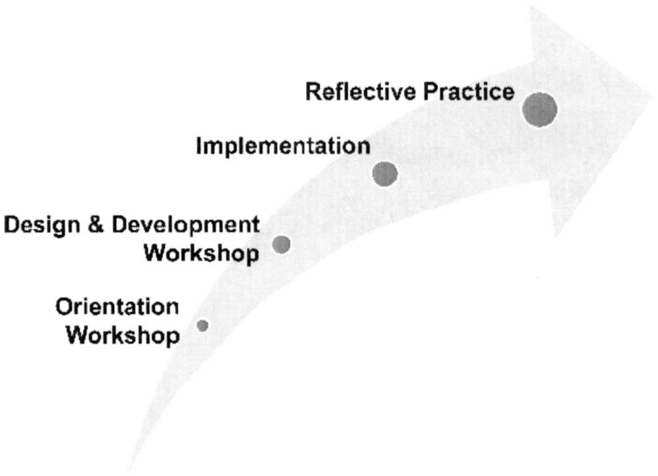

Reflective Practice

Implementation

Design & Development
Workshop

Orientation
Workshop

Four distinctly different training events have been designed to help teachers understand, implement and disseminate the teaching methods inherent in the PBCL process.

The first professional development activity is an _Orientation Workshop_. The intent of this workshop is to familiarize instructors, administrators and business partners to the PBCL process. This can be done with either an on-site, three-hour training program or an on-line version of the same program. In this workshop, teachers will discover what PBCL is, how it works, and why research findings have demonstrated it value in science, technology, engineering, and mathematics (STEM) education.

A second level of training is an intensive, fifteen-hour, face-to-face experience with instructors and business partners in an immersion experience in PBCL called _Design and Development Workshop_. An on-line version of the same program is also available. By the end of the institute participants will have designed their own PBCL pilot experiment. Participants will have investigated the underlying principles of the PBCL approach and practiced using processes and tools to design PBCL experiences and facilitate student teamwork. Business partners plan an important part in this training activity. They will be asked to work with teachers to define a business problem that can be used as an example to develop using the PBCL process.

Discussions about *Implementation* best practices are held periodically. These discussions include practitioners from around the United States. This venue allows the participants to collaborate with a community of practice to share lessons learned and strategies that work, as well as to support colleagues that may need help, suggestions, or guidance.

The final step in the professional development process is Reflecting on the Implementation. It is this last step that engages the metacognitive process and aids in knowledge transfer. PBCL practitioners who have implemented their course design in the classroom have likely benefited from the support of a PBCL mentor or the community as a whole, either personally or through available online support forums.

The *Reflection* is a written piece in the form of a blog article on Making Learning Real blog, or a published academic paper. These reflective pieces prepare PBCL practitioners to communicate their knowledge and skills in preparation for mentoring others in the practices of Problem-Based Case Learning.

The following portions of this chapter contain case studies of two individuals who have become expert teachers of the PBCL model. Their case studies tell of the process and rewards of becoming a PBCL mentor and being prepared to not only use the PBCL process in your classes but also to assist colleagues in learning to use the PBCL process.

Teacher-Trainers' Perspectives/Observations

Gail Malone

Gail Malone is Director of the Teaching and Learning Center at South Plains College, a community college in Texas. The center provides academic support, developmental instruction in reading, education courses, and faculty development for the West Texas community college. Five years ago the State of Texas provided funding for a 21st Century Problem Solving initiative, and Gail participated in the training. During that time, she was introduced to problem-based case learning. After two years of training, her task was to teach the faculty what she had learned and to work as a consultant with the teachers, observing in their classrooms and helping them to develop their own curriculum. Gail relates many success stories from those classes.

Like many teachers who are at a starting point of implementing PBCL, the faculty at South Plains did not always have a business partner. An exciting aspect of PBCL as practiced at South Plains is that faculty developed cases across the curriculum. Several classes in arts and sciences, including developmental reading, participated. One class analyzed political campaigns, using a local candidate as their business partner. The "real-world" learning experience came from working with the candidate to develop his campaign. Students wrote public service announcements for radio and television ads, wrote position papers, and composed and recorded a campaign theme song, among other activities.

Another class looked at security on the main campus following a student stabbing incident in the campus parking lot the preceding semester. They analyzed pertinent security issues, interviewed people in law enforcement, and researched security alert/monitoring systems. They developed proficiency not only in reading, but in using resources and making inferences as they worked toward recommendations to present to the college administration. "We were impressed by the eloquence of their oral presentations," Gail says. The developmental reading students were elated when the administration actually implemented one of their recommendations as a means of handling some of the security problems on campus.

By using a version of the Learning Cycle that put the emphasis on "thinking," students were able to integrate the skills for developmental reading, as identified through the Texas Success Initiative, specifically main ideas, details, vocabulary development, author's point of view and purpose, organization and structure, and study skills. Then they were able to use these skills in application, analysis, synthesis, evaluation and creation (Bloom's taxonomy) in a real-world situation to address a serious and important matter in their own experience – campus life.

In a sophomore level multi-culture course, education students used PBCL methodology in a study of professional ethics for educators. The student teams researched stories of faculty members, mostly public school teachers, who got into serious trouble because of social networking. The teams had to decide how they, as responsible educators, would distinguish between appropriate and inappropriate behavior. In their presentations, not only did they make policy recommendations, but they discussed each situation in terms of Bloom's Taxonomy. For example, they discussed the application, analysis/synthesis, evaluation of each problem example and then created possible policy recommendations or personal attitudes/behaviors that could avoid or prevent such problems. In other words, they described what happened, analyzed why that happened or how it happened, and how the situation could be avoided or eliminated, finally recommending what would be the best practice in the future.

"Their analysis was very reflective and revealed a real maturity of understanding and judgment, things we want to foster in our developing educators," says Gail.

She describes another class in which the case was built around campus violence. The question was posed: "What do you do when you witness an incident of violence or destruction of property?" The students' answer was immediate: "Take a picture on my cell phone." The discussion evolved into questions of privacy. Gail anticipated that students would be concerned about privacy issues, but they wanted security cameras everywhere, at all times. More in-depth conversation took place as they discussed the fact that students with criminal records were allowed to attend classes. Even if the offenders have a history of violence, their privacy is protected.

"Students thought faculty and students should be informed," Gail said. "I didn't anticipate the students' point of view. They were thinking in a way they'd never had to do before, considering multiple viewpoints and actually reflecting on how practices affected their own lives." This connected to another topic in the curriculum about the role of emotional intelligence in learning. Students placed safety at a much higher premium than privacy. This was in sharp contrast to the attitudes of many faculty and administrators who grew up in an era of "Big Brother is watching you," creating a sense of wariness. Students were much less concerned about individual privacy than they were about collective safety. Even basic civil rights were not as important as collective safety. These students who were for the most part in elementary school when the World Trade Center towers fell were acutely aware of and willing to sacrifice personal privacy to attain some level of protection.

There are textbooks that present realistic problems for students to consider, Gail points out, but when students have to dig on their own to address authentic situations, "it hits home."

Gail gives much credit to the outstanding faculty members who have participated in PBCL at South Plains. "They were identified, initially, because they taught high-risk courses. They were exceptional teachers - innovative, not afraid to use technology and not hesitant to try something new," she explains. Faculty were compensated for their work through a federal grant initiative to use technology for supplemental instruction and support, which often was achieved by faculty creating online support material and instructional aids. Faculty spent hours developing great online resources that students did not actually use, saying they didn't have time. On the other hand, when teachers utilized the PBCL approach, class time was allotted for interviewing, researching databases, developing presentation scenarios and programs, and so forth. In the PBCL, students were actually using the tools the teachers introduced, such as the Need-to-Know Board and the PBCL design tools, so there was a real sense that the time spent on the projects was very productive.

Faculty at South Plains College are still experimenting with PBCL. The outcomes aren't always one-hundred percent successful, but progress is usually noted in some areas. In a developmental learning community, students used "Water" as the problem for one unit of study. The Learning Community was a single cohort of students all needing developmental education in all three academic areas, and enrolled in the same developmental reading, developmental writing, developmental math and learning frameworks course, resulting in 12 semester credit hours total. This cohort group formed the Learning Community. In reading, the group read about and researched various topics concerning water (purity, cost, conservation, consumption, advertising, etc.); in writing, they wrote about what they had researched; in math, they did actual water analyses, using formulas to assess water purity and contamination, calculated the relative cost of bottled waters, assessed the impact of the bottled water industry on the national economy and the costs of plastic water bottle disposal on the environment, and so forth.

Since the cohort was an exceptionally weak group, needing developmental education in all three basic academic skills (and less than 5% of the total college population is weak in all three areas), the faculty were somewhat disappointed that the cohort did not perform better on tests than the control sample. Gail adds, "This might have been expected, considering the weak entry skills of this cohort." However, the group was very cohesive and course completion rates, persistence and retention were improved. The faculty were willing to try the concept again, suggesting that maybe the cohort be formed by linking reading and writing (and eliminating the math component).

In another instance, one instructor hasn't had success with her PBCL experiences though she has tried several. "I think it's just a matter of finding the right 'hook'," Gail explains. The developmental reading teacher tried one case about alternative energy sources to replace fossil fuels. "It was just too complex," Gail says. But the teacher knows "the PBCL theory is sound and the concept is strong. She keeps trying. The secret to success may be in identifying exactly what students care about most deeply."

Erika Volker

Erika Volker's journey through problem-based case learning (PBCL) began at the University of Northern Iowa Teacher Education program in Cedar Falls, Iowa. During the training, she was taught to teach using thematic and experiential learning techniques. From a student's perspective, that made a lot of sense to Erika. However, when she did her practicum experiences, her supervising teachers taught the traditional methods and relied on the textbooks to craft their lessons. Ericka says, "I found this very discouraging."

After graduation, she taught nutrition and money management skills to Food Stamp recipients through a co-op extension program, funded by a USDA Education grant. She was instructed to use a "canned" presentation. She had neither the opportunity nor the contact time to deliver thematic or inquiry-based instruction.

After she graduated with her Master's degree and began teaching at Metropolitan Community College as the Tech Prep, Dual Credit and Career Academy Coordinator, she was invited to attend a professional development experience called Problem-Based Case Learning at another community college. It was there that she found a group of "like-minded thought leaders." She worked in a team to craft an experiential learning unit for the Information Technology program. Erika recalls that these educators "reinforced all that I believed in regards to experiential and inquiry-based learning."

She took a position with the Omaha Chamber of Commerce, still excited about PBCL. She wrote and received a grant to conduct a five day PBCL workshop for high school teachers. To participate in the workshop the instructors had to come in a team, one academic and one Career and Technical education (CTE) teacher. That workshop resulted in others, and a trainer came out of the workshops.

PBCL has introduced Erika to internationally renowned "thought leaders" and helped her understand the needs of students in the 21st Century classroom and work environment. While she worked with the Omaha Chamber, the Skills Commission came out with the Jobs Pyramid. "It was then that I saw the direct correlation between higher order thinking skills and economic development," Erika says. "If our country is to stay economically strong, we MUST not teach knowledge-based information. We are in an ever changing world which requires problem solving, not regurgitation of facts and figures."

Erika is now the Director of Partnerships for Innovation (PFI). She manages ten percent of the Perkins grant funding in the state of Nebraska. As a part of her work over the past two years, PBCL has been a standard budget line item. Each of the partnering high schools and community colleges that contribute to PFI is provided PBCL training free-of-charge.

At this point in her journey through PBCL, Erika says, "PBCL has not only afforded me the opportunity to meet new people, reinforce my pedagogical beliefs, but has stretched my abilities professionally and personally. I am considered a subject matter expert in Nebraska as it relates to the 21st Century workforce preparation and I feel that PBCL was a great catalyst for my learning in this area."

7

WHERE DO WE GO FROM HERE

Over the past several years a revolution has been quietly at work in schools and classrooms across the nation. The revolution is changing the curriculum by having business partners provide input to the students and teachers in the form of real problems faced by their business. These real problems are designed to make learning real, meaningful and active for students. Hopefully, this revolution will make the connection between the classroom and the world-of-work more dynamic and productive. The process may be known by several different names including problem-based leaning, project-based learning or any similar descriptive title.

When this project staff started the series of projects described in this book, we investigated the similarities and differences between these techniques. Each of them intended to make education more relevant to the students and to get students more actively involved in the learning process. We heartily support all of these efforts and encourage teachers to use these techniques. However, as we were studying the processes, we realized that the final customer was often missing from the discussions. Where was the business partner? Of course, some teachers do consult with business people when designing problems or projects, but that number is extremely small.

As we started this series of NSF projects, we wanted to make learning real, active, and engaging. Not only did we want students engaged with the technology of the problem but we wanted them to be engaged with real environments in which these projects exist. It was obvious that problems designed by book publishers or even by many teachers are simplified by eliminating the total environment in which the problem existed. The reason for this is obvious.

Problems were to illustrate a single point or concept and were thus intended to amplify lessons presented in a textbook or a lecture. However, problems taken out of context are seldom useful nor do they prepare students for the conditions under which problems exist on the job. At most, typical problems that students are asked to solve do little more than illustrate concepts presented in a lecture.

Problem-Based Case Learning (PBCL), as discussed in the previous chapters, changes the typical classroom into one of discussion, team activities, outside research, data gathering, and communicating with fellow students, teachers, and business partners. Students encounter problems within the real, business environment in which they exist. It is extremely important for students to learn that environment as well as technical concepts.

One of the most encouraging results of the PBCL projects has been the comments from employers of graduates who had PBCL processes incorporated within their classes. Without exception, employers have mentioned that students who had worked on PBCL problems were better equipped to begin their new jobs. They were more familiar with working in teams, solving problems as a group, considering economics and other business conditions, and making presentations to other workers while working under deadlines. New employees who had worked with PBCL as students were able to be productive on their new jobs months faster than students who were hired in the past and who were taught with more traditional teaching techniques.

The name problem-based case learning is actually very descriptive of the process. The learning takes place around a problematic situation based on a local business. The word "case" is included in the description but is not to be confused with the process of "case studies." A case study is a post-mortem of a situation that has already happened. A case study is based on an historical even or happening. Case studies have been used effectively in many fields of education such as is done in the legal profession.

However, in this series of projects the term "Case Files" has been applied to illustrate that the problem is a real event but is currently happening and has never been solved previously. Therefore, groups of students can be working on the same problem but come to different conclusions and recommendations. Unlike case studies, case files have no one right answer. Each student group may suggest a different solution that is equally valid.

The reason PBCL is such a powerful learning technique is defined in the book edited by Dr. Bransford where he calls out three critical components to the learning environment: prior knowledge, deep understanding, and metacognition. As is pointed out in that book, each person presented with a problem envisions a solution which is based upon his or her past experiences. Regardless of age and background, we all have preconceived ideas about a problem that are based on our personal experiences. Since everyone has different experiences, working in the team allows students to share their experiences relative to the problem they are facing.

PBCL allows students to use their background of experiences while traditional lecture methods of teaching asks students to disregard their past experiences and learn the material the way it is presented. Unfortunately, most people cannot disregard their experiences and as a result are often confused or unable to learn the material the way it is presented. Allowing them to build on their background of experience and to share it with others is one of the strongest advantages of the PBCL process.

Students learn new material in many different ways. Teachers using the PBCL process must be aware of the different ways in which their students learn and allow them to use the processes best suited to them. Some students learn best by reading and thinking about a subject while others learn best by discussing the concept with other students. The Learning Cycle used within the PBCL process allows each student to learn in the best way for them. It may be library research or it may be discussions with a knowledgeable person such as the teacher or the business partner that helps the student comprehend new knowledge. Still others may need to "see" the process in action.

We all know how valuable field trips can be when properly planned. Perhaps a student needs to observe a similar process at a business or other location while preparing to study the problem. Many times, consulting with the instructor on a one-on-one basis can help the student gain new knowledge about the process. This is also a time when the student can assimilate information from many sources including other classes, other students and teachers.

A concept from a past math or science class may be a connecting link for the student to gain new knowledge related to the problem being faced. Since students learn new material in different ways, we want to provide them opportunities to learn the new materials in the most effective way for them individually. This cannot be accomplished with traditional lecture methods where the teacher decides upon the learning method to be used.

Metacognition means to think about thinking. Asking students to write a review of what has been studied allows them to think about what they have been doing and what they have been learning. It is far more than a review of the process. Instead, students are asked to bring the facts then have discovered together and evaluate how they have solved the problem. Typically, preparing to give a presentation to others about the plan, process and discoveries they have made helps them to organize their thoughts on the subject and forces them to integrate all the components of the problem that they have uncovered in such a way that others, teachers, business partners and students can understand what they did and why they believe they have identified the best solution to the problem.

PBCL presents a challenge to the student, but teachers are also challenged to learn a new teaching technique. Instead of being content or technology focused, the teacher has to be equipped to guide the students in their learning process. After all, student learning, not teachers presenting, is the focus and the goal of education. Thus, frequently teachers must be willing to adapt to a new style of educational leadership.

First of all the teacher must seek out a business partner who is willing and able to share a real problem faced by their organization. Once that is accomplished the teacher must adapt the business, possibly with the assistance of the business partner, to be recognized by students in the classroom as an interesting challenge to accept. Selling the importance of the problem and how it relates to the topic of the class is essential for teachers to do, but they must not divulge an anticipated solution. The teacher's role is to encourage and excite students about the importance of the problem.

Once the problem is introduced to the students, the teacher serves as the "guide on the side." Without telling the students how to solve the problem, the teacher needs to help the students channel their thinking toward resources that will lead to developing a solution. Students should be encouraged to consult books, government records or documents, interviews with people involved with the process, web research and countless other resources.

Not all students need to use the same resources, but, as a team, students should share what they learn with each other. As the students gather their research and begin to understand the problem and formulate a solution, it is sometimes necessary for the teacher to introduce a new concept. An illustration of this is used in the Introduction to Engineering Technology course at Nashville State.

As students gather data to solve a problem, a computer tool such as a spreadsheet has been found to be very helpful. The teacher may take the students on a short side trip and give them basic instructions on how to use a spreadsheet to solve an equation and to draw a graph of data. In that short (one or two day) side trip students can become functional with the basics of spreadsheets and can use them to help solve simple equations with associated graphical information. Students are then encouraged to use a spreadsheet if it can assist them in solving their assigned problem. If not for the current problem, students will be able to use a spreadsheet as a tool to help solve future problems.

Frequently, within a given class or even a small group of students, there is a student who has experience with spreadsheets and can use his or her prior knowledge to assist other students. Students learning from other students is often more effective than direct intervention from the teacher.

As the problem solution matures and students work their way around The Learning Cycle shown in Figure 3, they need to review what the original objective was, as defined by the business partner in the initial step.

- Are they working toward a desired solution or has their research and data collection taken them off track?

- Have they considered all of the items expressed by the business partner when the problem was first introduced?
- Have they considered the technical aspects of the problem?
- Have they considered other aspects such as cost,
- productivity, ability to integrate the solution in existing company operations?
- In short, will their proposed solution work?
- Is their research based on fact or on "hearsay"?
- Will their proposed solution work in the environment that was originally defined?

As the final phase of the problem, the team must put their ideas together in a meaningful presentation designed to inform the business partner and the teacher of their proposed solution. All students should share in this team responsibility. Many students want to avoid being in front of a group and speaking. Even though this can be very difficult, emotionally, students need to learn how to present a justification for their work.

Very few businesses allow students to work in a vacuum. Instead, they must communicate their ideas to other workers and their management. This step in the Learning Cycle should not be shortchanged or avoided. It is much easier for a shy student to learn to make a presentation before his colleagues and other students than to have his first experience with a presentation in front of an employer.

Some technical teachers have found it helpful to invite a colleague from the English or speech department to come to the student presentations. In fact, if the teachers from the English or speech department are willing to council the teams of students while they are preparing their presentations, it is very meaningful to the students and helps them to realize how important academic subjects are to the success of technical endeavors.

Several teacher training activities have been conducted as part of the past projects in this series. Project team members continue to hold training seminars for teachers interested in learning the PBCL methods of teaching. In addition, the project web site, www.makinglearningreal. org, has several tutorial programs available for teachers to learn the process. Teachers experienced with the PBCL process are also available to serve as mentors for other teachers attempting to apply the PBCL process to their classes.

The project team wishes to thank Dr. George Van Allen, President of Nashville State Community College, for his willingness to provide release time for one of the experienced PBCL developers and teachers to maintain the project web site and to provide assistance with mentoring other teachers from around the nation as funding from NSF for this activity ends. This type of commitment will assure that Problem-Based Case Learning will continue to expand in the nation's classrooms.

REFERENCES

Bereiter, C., & Scardamalia, M. (1993). Surpassing Ourselves: An Inquiry into the Nature and Implications of Expertise, Chicago, IL: Open Court.

Bransford, J. D. (2007, January). Preparing people for rapidly changing environments. Journal of Engineering Education, 1-3.

Bransford, J.D. & Schwartz, D. (1999). Rethinking transfer: A simple proposal with multiple implications. In A. Iran-

Nejad & P. D. Pearson (Eds.), Review of Research in Education (Vol. 24 pp. 61-100). Washington, DC: American Educational Research Association.

Bransford, J. D., & Schwartz, D. (2009). It takes expertise to make expertise: Some thoughts about why and how and reflections on themes in chapters 15-18. In K. Anders Ericsson (Ed.), Development of professional expertise (pp.432-448). New York: Cambridge.

Bransford, J., Copland, M., Honig, M., Nelson, H. G., Mosborg, S., Gawel, D., Phillips, R. S., & Vye, N. (2010). Adaptive people and adaptive systems: Issue of learning and design. In A. Hargreaves, M. Fullan, D. Hopkins, & A. Leiberman (Eds.), The second international handbook of educational change (pp.825-826). Dordrect, The Netherlands: Springer.

Bransford, J., Brown, A., & Cocking, R., editors (2000). How People Learn: Brain, Mind, Experience and School. Committee on Developments in the Science of Learning. National Academy Press.

College Board (2008). Winning the Skills Race and Strengthening America's Middle Class: An Action Agenda for Community Colleges. [http://professionals.collegeboard.com/ profdownload/winning_the_skills_race.pdf]

Ericsson, K. A. (2009). Development of Professional Expertise. New York: Cambridge.

Gragg, C. I. (1940, October). Because wisdom can't be told. Harvard Alumni Bulletin, 78-84.

Hatano, G., & Inagaki, K. (1986). Two courses of expertise. In H. Stevenson, H. Azuma, & K. Hakuta (Eds.), Child development and education in Japan (pp.262–272). NY: W.H. Freeman and Company.

Lin, X., Schwartz, D., Bransford, J. (2006). Intercultural adaptive expertise: Explicit and implicit lessons from Dr. Hatano. Human Development, 50, 65-72.

Kay, K., & Greenhill, V. (2011) 21st Century Education for Education Leaders, Boston, MA: Pearson.

Miller, R.B. (1978). The information system designer. In W.T. Singleton (Ed.), The Analysis of Practical Skills (pp. 278-291). Baltimore, MD: University Park Press.

Moore, Brooke, and Richard Parker (2001). Critical Thinking. 6th ed. Mountain View: Mayfield.

Parker, W. C. (2010). Listening to strangers: Classroom discussion in democratic education. Teachers College Record, 112(11), 2815–2832.

Robinson, A. G., & Stern, S. (1998). Corporate Creativity. San Francisco, CA: Berrett-Koehler, Publishers.

Rose, M. (2004). The Mind at Work: Valuing the Intelligence of the American Worker. New York: Penguin.

Shutt, K., Phillips, R. S., Vye, N. J., Van Horne, K., & Bransford, J. D. (2010). Developing science inquiry skills with challenge-based student-directed learning. Paper presented at the American Educational Research Association.

Williams, S. M. (1992). Putting case-based instruction into context: Examples from legal and medical education. Journal of the Learning Sciences, 2(4), 367–427.

Online References

The Making Learning Real:
        http://www.makinglearningreal.org

The Nashville State Community College Critical Thinking Initiative:
        http://ww2.nscc.edu/think/

The Case Files:
        http://www.thecasefiles.org

Model Cases from SEATEC:
        http://www.thecasefiles.org/PBCS-ModelCases3.htm

Institute for Habits of Mind/Art Costa:
        http://www.instituteforhabitsofmind.com/

The Shopping Cart/Deep Dive from ABC's Nightline:
        http://www.youtube.com/watch?v=M66ZU2PCIcM